THE MESSENGER OF LIGHT

3I/ATLAS AND THE AWAKENING OF DIVINE RESONANCE

Tina Ketch

THE MESSENGER OF LIGHT
3I/ATLAS AND THE AWAKENING OF DIVINE RESONANCE

This book is a work of spiritual reflection. While it draws on scientific concepts and historical references, it is intended for inspirational and educational purposes only. The interpretations and perspectives expressed are those of the author and should not be considered scientific or theological doctrine.

ISBN: 979-8-9937372-0-1
eISBN: 979-8-9937372-1-8
For information, inquiries, or permissions, contact:

https://TinaKetch.com
TinaKetch@me.com
https://YouTube.com/TinaKetch

DEDICATION

To the Travelers of Light, those who gaze at the heavens and feel the pulse of something greater, those who have looked for love in silence and found it shining back through the stars.

To the hearts that still wonder, to the souls that still seek, and to the ones who listen for the divine hum beneath creation, this book is for you.

May the light that called the comet into motion awaken the same remembrance within you: that you are not separate from the stars, but born of their radiance, guided by the same eternal hand that moves galaxies, hearts, and grace itself.

And to the Source of all resonance, the Christ Light that breathes through every world, this work is my humble offering of love.

- Tina Ketch

TABLE OF CONTENTS

PREFACE

There are moments in history when the universe itself speaks, not in words, but in movement, in light, in the silent language of vibration. One such moment occurred when an interstellar traveler, known to astronomers as **3I/ATLAS**, entered our solar system. To science, it was a visitor from beyond the stars; to the soul, it was a messenger, a reminder that all of creation is alive, interconnected, and resonant with divine intelligence.

This book began as a simple curiosity: What does it mean when something not born of our solar system passes through it? Yet as I studied the orbit, light patterns, and the harmonics of its trajectory, a deeper question emerged: What message does creation whisper through such motion?

For me, **3I/ATLAS** became more than a comet; it became a revelation. It's passing illuminated the truth that everything in existence vibrates with purpose. Every planet, every heart, every breath participates in the same symphony of light. And in that harmony, we are not alone. We never have been.

This book is not a scientific analysis, though it honors science. It is a spiritual reflection, a journey into how the universe mirrors the human soul. Just as **3I/ATLAS** moved through the solar system, awakening resonance in the celestial spheres, so too does divine energy move through each of us, awakening memory, awareness, and grace.

The Messenger of Light invites you to see the cosmos not as distant, but as intimate. To hear vibration not as an abstract frequency, but as the living Word of God in motion. To recognize that when the heavens stir, the soul remembers.

This is a story of light meeting light, the celestial and the human, the infinite and the intimate, converging in a single, radiant truth: all that moves, moves with love. - Tina Ketch

INTRODUCTION

THE CELESTIAL VOICE, WHEN THE UNIVERSE SPEAKS THROUGH MOTION

Long before telescopes, humankind looked to the stars and understood, instinctively, that the heavens were not silent. The ancients read the language of light and movement as scripture written across the sky, with every planet a syllable and every orbit a verse.

Today, we have telescopes and data, yet the mystery remains. For when a body like **3I/ATLAS** enters our solar system, not from within, but from the depths of interstellar space, something within us stirs. Something ancient. Something eternal.

It is as though the universe itself sends a messenger to remind us: You are not separate from creation; you are creation remembering itself.

The journey of **3I/ATLAS** became, for me, a mirror of the soul's own passage, a sacred metaphor for awakening. It traveled from the unknown, passed near our sun, the source of all life and illumination, and continued on its infinite path. Isn't that our story too? To come from the divine source, to enter the radiant field of consciousness, and to journey onward, ever-expanding in light?

The Vibrational Universe

Modern physics tells us that everything in existence vibrates. From the smallest quantum particle to the grand sweep of galaxies, all reality is motion, frequency, resonance. The Bible calls this The Word. *"In the beginning was the Word,"* writes John 1:1, *"and the Word was with God, and the Word was God."*

What if that Word was vibration itself? What if the voice of God is not sound, but frequency, the invisible hum sustaining everything that is?

When we think of a comet, we imagine ice and dust, but energetically, it is a moving instrument. As it passes planets, its field interacts with the planets' fields. Gravitationally, magnetically, and spiritually, it sends ripples through the solar web. Each planet, in turn, adjusts its subtle vibrational tone, like strings of a cosmic harp responding to a single pluck.

Now imagine the same principle within you. Every thought, emotion, and intention sends its own vibrational current into the universe. Just as the planets adjust to celestial motion, your soul adjusts to inner movement. What you feel, you broadcast. What you love, you amplify.

And so, when something as rare as **3I/ATLAS** enters the field of our solar system, it is not only a celestial event, it is an invitation. It invites us to remember that the universe is alive, and that we are participants in its unfolding resonance.

The Divine Mirror

The heavens are not outside of us; they are reflected within us. Each planet corresponds to an aspect of the soul: courage, compassion, wisdom, reflection, and transformation. The stars mirror our higher nature, reminding us of the light we carry but often forget to see.

When **3I/ATLAS** appeared, it was like a traveler crossing not only space but consciousness, a spark igniting awareness in those ready to listen. Its brilliance was not accidental. It was a demonstration of divine orchestration, the universe revealing that even what seems foreign or unfamiliar can carry light.

In the language of energy, we might say that **3I/ATLAS** enhanced the vibrational tone of the planets as it passed them, subtle, unseen harmonics awakening new frequencies of awareness. In the language of spirit, we might say: Heaven moved, and Earth responded.

Just as tides respond to the gravitational pull of the moon, consciousness responds to the cosmic movement. You may have felt it as restlessness, awakening, sudden insight, or the return of long-forgotten emotions. When the heavens shift, the inner world stirs. When light passes, memory awakens.

The Message of Motion

Everything that moves carries a message. A comet's arc, a planet's orbit, the turning of seasons, all reflect divine intelligence at work.

3I/ATLAS, in particular, came as a reminder that we are not static beings bound to one timeline or one solar field. Like that visitor, our souls, too, are interstellar, born from divine light, traveling through dimensions of growth and remembrance.

The same divine spark that called that comet into motion calls you to rise, to awaken, to move through fear, through shadow, through time itself, back to the awareness of your own eternal resonance.

When the Universe Moves, the Soul Responds

You were made to feel these cosmic tides. The same vibrational force that stirs planets stirs the heart. The same field that holds galaxies together holds you in its luminous embrace.

When a celestial body crosses our skies, it is not random; it is a revelation. It is the universe saying, 'Pay attention.' Something within you is aligning with something beyond you.

The appearance of **3I/ATLAS** was a visible echo of the invisible truth: that the divine is never silent, never absent, and never far away. We are living in an era when heaven speaks not only through Scripture but through science, not only through prophets, but through patterns of light.

Every orbit, every vibration, every breath, every prayer, all part of the same universal rhythm.

This is the story that unfolds in these pages: how motion becomes message, how vibration becomes revelation, and how love, always love, is the final frequency through which all creation returns home.

"The heavens declare the glory of God; the skies proclaim the work of His hands. ", Psalm 19:1

THE VISITOR AND THE VIBRATION OF GRACE

THE CELESTIAL MESSENGER

There are moments when the universe speaks in light rather than words, when something vast and ancient moves through the dark and stirs the soul of creation. When astronomers discovered **3I/ATLAS**, the interstellar traveler moving through our solar system, it became more than a scientific curiosity. It was a message, a movement, a reminder that the universe is alive with rhythm, a rhythm set long before time began.

It came silently, streaking through the void, untouched by any sun or system. It passed through the family of planets like a note in an eternal song, faint, brief, but perfectly in tune. And perhaps that was its purpose: to remind us that nothing in creation is random. Every orbit, every collision, every flicker of starlight carries intention.

To the scientist, **3I/ATLAS** is a body of dust and ice, a wanderer from another star. To the mystic, it is something more: a celestial messenger, a visitor carrying the vibrational memory of other worlds, other suns, and the divine spark that set them all in motion.

The heavens, after all, are not still. They breathe. They sing. They move in circles so vast that our lives are but a heartbeat within their measure. And yet, we are part of that same symphony.

"Lift up your eyes on high and see: who created these? He who brings out their host by number, calling them all by name. ", Isaiah 40:26

Each star is a word. Each planet is a phrase. Each comet is a sentence in the ongoing revelation of divine creation. And perhaps **3I/ATLAS** was one such phrase, brief, radiant, uttered only once, but carrying meaning enough to awaken wonder across the cosmos.

The Language of Motion

In the beginning, there was vibration. Before there was form or sound or light, there was the Word, the divine frequency through which all things came into being. *"Let there be light"* was not only a declaration, but also a resonance. Creation began with the movement of energy, the first wave of intention pulsing through the infinite.

Everything that exists vibrates. Every atom hums with life. Every star and planet spins in sacred rhythm, held together by invisible frequencies that mirror the music of the divine.

What science calls gravity, the spirit might call grace, an unseen bond of attraction that holds all things in relationship, each moving in harmony with the rest. It is the choreography of love itself.

When the interstellar traveler **3I/ATLAS** entered this field, it joined the rhythm, however briefly, and its motion, its speed, its luminous tail became part of the universal choir. A note so high it could not be heard, so vast it could only be felt.

Perhaps that is what the heavens were teaching us: that motion itself is praise. That even the tiniest particle, in its orbit, is singing its devotion to the Source. And that the same divine resonance that moves the galaxies also moves through the human heart.

For within each of us is a reflection of that same design, the same pulsing geometry, the same harmonic ratio of energy and rest. Our breath mirrors the tides. Our heartbeat echoes the rhythm of the planets. Our thoughts ripple outward like radio waves through the unseen.

We are not apart from the cosmos; we are its consciousness made flesh. We are how the universe knows itself in love.

And so when a traveler like **3I/ATLAS** glides through the great sea of creation, something inside us remembers. It stirs the ancient recognition that we, too, are travelers, carriers of divine light, shaped by motion, called by resonance. We are living vibrations in the eternal song of grace.

The Resonance of the Planets

Every planet hums with its own vibration. Science measures this as electromagnetic resonance, subtle oscillations in magnetic fields and solar winds, but the mystic hears it as music. It is said that if one could listen beyond sound, the universe would reveal itself as a symphony: each celestial body contributing its own note to the eternal harmony of creation.

Earth sings at a frequency known as the Schumann Resonance, a low, rhythmic pulse that mirrors the human heartbeat at rest. Venus vibrates softly, like a hymn of devotion. Jupiter thunders in the deep bass tones of power and wisdom. And Saturn, the keeper of time, hums the song of structure and consequence.

Together they form what the ancients called the Music of the Spheres, a divine composition too vast for human ears but deeply felt by the soul.

This resonance is not abstract. It is the pulse of grace that holds galaxies together. It is the rhythm of divine order, the breath of God made audible through motion.

"The heavens declare the glory of God; the skies proclaim the work of His hands. ", Psalm 19:1

When we look to the heavens and sense their beauty, what we are feeling is resonance. Our spirits vibrate in sympathy with the song of the stars. We are instruments in the orchestra of creation, and when we fall silent, when fear, pain, or disconnection muffle our tone, we forget that we are part of that grand harmony.

But grace is patient. It does not demand that we play perfectly, only that we remember the music.

When a traveler like **3I/ATLAS** passes through the cosmic field, it does not come as an intruder but as a reminder. Its movement ripples through the frequencies of the planets, and through them, into the soul of humankind. Not as a catastrophe, but as an invitation. Not as a change from without, but awakening from within.

Perhaps its passage called us to tune again, to realign our hearts with the original vibration of love. For the universe is not a void; it is a choir. And every being, seen or unseen, belongs to the song.

When Heaven Moves, Earth Responds

The movements of heaven are not isolated from the movements of earth. When the planets shift, when comets cross, when solar winds rise, the magnetic field of the earth responds. Winds change. Tides breathe differently. Even the human body, attuned to these subtle patterns, feels the stirrings of unseen motion.

Science can measure only a fraction of this dance, but the heart feels it entirely. When the air grows heavy before a storm, or when a sunrise feels unusually sacred, what we experience is resonance, the body recognizing the pulse of heaven in its own blood.

So it is with **3I/ATLAS** and all celestial movement. We are not passive witnesses of the cosmos; we are participants. Every wave of light, every whisper of magnetism passes through us. Our hearts, rich with iron and frequency, respond in kind.

It is no accident that ancient prophets watched the skies for signs, or that wise ones marked sacred days by the movement of stars. They understood that the divine speaks through order and rhythm, not as superstition, but as relationship. Heaven and Earth were not separate realms, but mirrors of the same truth: that all creation moves as one body, guided by one eternal pulse.

"He stretches out the north over the void and hangs the earth on nothing.", Job 26:7

To the heart that listens, every movement above mirrors a movement within. When a new star is born, a new awareness stirs in the soul of humanity. When a comet passes, a forgotten memory awakens, the remembrance that we, too, are made of light. When the heavens tremble, prayer deepens. When the universe exhales, we feel it as a gift of grace.

The wind, the tides, the breath, all follow the same rhythm. So does love. It flows, it expands, it returns. And like **3I/ATLAS**, it may vanish from view for a time, only to remind us that it was never gone, only passing through a more expansive sky.

The Inner Cosmos

The vastness of the heavens is mirrored within you. Every neuron that sparks in the mind, every pulse that beats within the chest, every breath that moves through the lungs, all echo the structure of creation itself. The ancients knew this when they spoke of humanity being made in the image of God. It was not only likeness in form, but in function, that the body and spirit would serve as microcosms of the divine order.

When you close your eyes and listen deeply, you can feel it: the quiet hum of your own being. The rhythm of your breath becomes the turning of the Earth. The pulse in your wrist becomes the heartbeat of stars. And in that awareness, the boundary between heaven and earth dissolves. You realize that what you thought was distant, the divine, the cosmic, the infinite, has been pulsing within you all along.

"For indeed, the kingdom of God is within you. ", Luke 17:21

You are the universe remembering itself through human form. You are light condensed into consciousness. You are breath made holy by awareness.

Your cells shimmer with the identical particles that once burned in ancient stars. Your DNA spirals like galaxies in miniature, each strand singing the same silent hymn that holds the planets in orbit. And the love that birthed creation is the same love that animates your heart.

When you feel disconnected, when Jesus feels far away, it is not because He has gone anywhere. It is because the static of the world has filled the signal. You have not been abandoned; you have been distracted. The light has not left you, only dimmed beneath the noise.

To return is simple: Breathe. Listen. Remember.

Each breath you take is the breath of God moving through form. Each heartbeat is the echo of divine rhythm. You are not seeking love; you are rediscovering the vibration that was there before the world began.

The Vibration of Christ Consciousness

The Gospel of John begins, *"In the beginning was the Word, and the Word was with God, and the Word was God."* That Word, the Logos, is not a spoken syllable. It is vibration, consciousness, divine frequency manifest. It is the song of creation made flesh in the person of Jesus Christ.

Christ is the divine vibration that holds all things together, the resonance that bridges the finite and the infinite, heaven and earth, body and spirit. To encounter Jesus is to experience the original sound of creation, the frequency of unconditional love.

When He spoke, the waves of His words carried healing. When He touched, His energy recalibrated what was dissonant. When He forgave, He transmuted pain into light. He was not performing miracles against the laws of nature. He was revealing them as they truly are: that love is the highest vibration, and everything returns to harmony when love is present.

"He is before all things, and in Him all things hold together.", Colossians 1:17

This is not a metaphor. It is metaphysics, the divine physics of being. Christ consciousness is the underlying order of the universe, the resonance of compassion and coherence that sustains all life. Every atom is His syllable; every heartbeat, His whisper.

When **3I/ATLAS** moves through the cosmic field, it is passing through Him, and because He is within you, the vibration passes through you as well. Each celestial movement, each wave of light, is another articulation of His eternal Word.

You are not apart from that Word; you are spoken by it. Every thought, emotion, and action vibrates in response to this divine speech. When you live in fear, you fall out of tune. When you live in love, you resonate again.

This is why prayer restores peace. Not because you are heard from afar, but because your vibration realigns with the Source within. In the silence of prayer, you tune back into Christ's frequency. You feel the hum of grace beneath your own skin, a vibration that is both infinitely personal and immeasurably vast.

When you love, you are broadcasting His signal into the world. When you forgive, you clear the static that once blocked it. When you create, you are echoing the act of Genesis, letting the divine frequency manifest through you.

Christ's love is not a feeling to chase. It is a state of resonance to return to. It is the still point in the spinning galaxy of your being, the magnetic center that draws all things toward balance. It does not demand perfection, only openness. It is constantly transmitting; we must only learn to receive.

Reflection

Close your eyes. Imagine a light deep within your chest, soft, golden, and steady. Let it expand with each breath until it fills your whole body. Now imagine that light flowing beyond you, into the world, into the stars, into the endless sky. See how it moves through every planet, every heart, every form.

This is the vibration of Christ, unbroken, eternal, everywhere at once. It hums through the bones of the Earth, through the wings of angels, through the pulse of every living thing. It is the voice that created all and sustains all. It is the music that will never cease.

You are part of that song. You are its melody, its breath, its beauty. And when you remember that truth, when you feel it in your chest, you will know without question: You have never been forgotten. You have always been loved. You have always been held in the vibration of Christ.

Living in the Field of Resonance

There is a stillness between the movements of the stars, a quiet heartbeat that keeps the whole of creation in rhythm. That stillness is grace. It exists between heaven and earth, between every inhale and exhale, between one heartbeat and the next. It is the divine pause through which the eternal breath of God passes, invisible, but felt by the soul that listens.

This same stillness lives in you. It hums beneath every thought and heartbeat, waiting for you to remember it. When you attune yourself to this inner field, when you let the noise fall away and open the heart to silence, you discover that you are not separate from creation. You are part of its pulse.

"Be still, and know that I am God.", Psalm 46:10

The heavens may swirl with endless motion, as comets pass, stars die, and galaxies are born, yet the center remains unchanged. That center is Christ. The unshakable axis around which all motion turns. He is the quiet inside every storm, the calm within every orbit. To dwell in Him is to rest in the field between worlds, the place where time and eternity meet, where all things find their rhythm again.

When **3I/ATLAS** passed through our solar system, it was not a disruption but a chord, a single note struck upon the vast instrument of creation. And perhaps, in its passage, it awakened in every soul the reminder that movement is not chaos, but communion, that everything in creation is in conversation with God.

You are part of that conversation. Your life, your choices, your thoughts, your breath, they ripple outward into the great field, shaping the resonance of humanity itself. Each act of kindness brightens the field. Each act of forgiveness strengthens it. Each prayer restores balance where fear once distorted the song.

The Breath That Unites Worlds

Every breath you take connects two realms: the visible and the invisible. When you inhale, you draw in the essence of creation, particles that once danced within stars, energy that has journeyed across eons. When you exhale, you give back that same essence, now infused with consciousness, gratitude, and love.

This is the rhythm of communion. The same flow that governs the tides, the rotation of planets, and the cycle of life itself. It is a sacred exchange, the universe breathing through you, and you through it.

To breathe with awareness is to pray without ceasing. Each breath says, *"Thy will be done."* Each exhale whispers, *"And let it be through me."*

As you breathe, imagine the love of Christ flowing in, radiant, alive, healing, filling your cells with light. Then, as you exhale, imagine that light flowing outward, to loved ones, to strangers, to the very edges of creation. You are not just breathing; you are participating in the ongoing act of divine creation.

"The Spirit of God has made me, and the breath of the Almighty gives me life.", Job 33:4

The Bridge of Light

Between heaven and earth, between spirit and matter, stands a bridge made of light, invisible, but eternal. Each soul that awakens to divine love becomes a point of brilliance along that bridge, a spark in the great network of grace. This is how heaven touches earth, through you, through me, through all who remember that love is not distant but dwelling within.

When you act in compassion, the bridge glows brighter. When you create from joy, it's current strengthens. When you forgive, when you speak peace, when you hold faith in the unseen, you extend the bridge farther still. Together, all awakened hearts form a living constellation, a spiritual circuitry of grace that hums with the light of Christ across the universe.

Every prayer ever spoken adds another beam of radiance to that sacred structure. Every act of mercy resonates across galaxies. You may think your kindness small, but the heavens record every vibration. Nothing is lost in love.

Prayer of Resonance

Lord of Light, Breath of Creation, let me live as one attuned to Your frequency. Let every word I speak and thought I hold harmonize with Your love.

When the world feels heavy, remind me of the rhythm beneath the noise.

When I lose my way, guide me by the music You placed in my soul.

When I forget Your nearness, breathe through me again until I remember.

Let my heartbeat echo the turning of Your stars, my breath rise and fall with the tides of Your grace.

And let this life, every step, every silence, be my hymn of gratitude to the One who holds all things in perfect vibration.

Reflection

Sit in stillness and place your hand over your heart. Feel the pulse beneath your fingers, steady, patient, alive. That rhythm is the echo of the same divine vibration that moves through the stars. You are not separate from the heavens. You are their continuation, their embodied resonance.

Let that knowing wash over you like light. You are the bridge between worlds. You are the sound of grace becoming flesh. You are the breath through which eternity speaks.

And when you walk in that awareness, you walk as one who knows the truth behind all creation: that Jesus is the vibration of love, and through Him, heaven and earth forever sing as one.

THE SUSTAINING LIGHT, LIVING IN DAILY RESONANCE

There are moments when you feel aligned, when peace hums softly in your chest, when the air feels light, and love flows without effort. You are in resonance then. You are living within the vibration of Christ. But the challenge is not simply to find that moment; it is to sustain it amid the noise, the schedules, and the countless small heartbreaks that try to pull you away.

Living in resonance is not about perfection. It is about awareness, the continual return to the divine rhythm that already holds you. It is remembering that Jesus does not step in and out of your life; He breathes through it. Your awareness of Him may fluctuate, but His love does not.

"In Him we live and move and have our being.", Acts 17:28

This truth means that every breath, every movement, every thought is sacred ground. When you move with love, you are in tune with creation. When you act with kindness, you amplify the frequency of Heaven on Earth. And when you forgive, you recalibrate your vibration to match that of grace itself.

The Physics of Presence

The body is more than matter; it is a repository of memory. Each cell remembers how you think, feel, and believe. When your thoughts are anxious, your cells tighten. When your heart is at peace, your body softens and opens.

Modern research calls this cellular resonance, yet the Bible has spoken of it for millennia:

"A cheerful heart is good medicine, but a crushed spirit dries up the bones.", Proverbs 17:22

Your inner state radiates outward. The electromagnetic field of your heart expands several feet beyond your body, interacting with the fields of others. When you walk into a room filled with gratitude, the atmosphere subtly but powerfully changes. This is why the presence of Jesus transformed people without words. He carried perfect coherence, divine vibration in human form. To stand near Him was to feel yourself remembered by love.

You carry a measure of that same energy. When your heart is anchored in peace, you emit the frequency of healing. When you pray, your vibration rises, harmonizing your body with spirit. When you speak with love, the air itself seems to shift.

To sustain resonance, cultivate presence. Breathe slowly. Speak gently. Pause often. Each moment of still awareness invites grace to flow unobstructed through your life.

The Practice of Alignment

The world around you vibrates with noise, both emotional and mental, as well as digital. It pulls at your frequency like static distorting a signal. To maintain divine coherence, you must become the tuning fork that returns all things to harmony.

Three sacred practices anchor your vibration: gratitude, service, and silence.

1. Gratitude recalibrates your perception. It shifts the frequency of your thoughts from one of lack to one of abundance, from fear to faith. Every thank you whispered from the heart sends a wave of healing through your body and outward into creation. *"Give thanks in all circumstances; for this is God's will for you in Christ Jesus. "*, 1 Thessalonians 5:18
2. Service grounds light into form. Every act of kindness stabilizes your energy field. When you help a stranger, comfort a friend, or care for the earth, you become a conduit for divine order. Service is love given direction, vibration given purpose.

3. Silence restores your natural rhythm. In stillness, the nervous system resets. The heart synchronizes with the Earth's resonance, and you hear again the voice that speaks beneath all noise: *"Be still, and know that I am God."*

Emotional Stewardship

To sustain high vibration is not to avoid emotion, but to transform it. Jesus did not deny His sorrow in Gethsemane; He transmuted it through surrender. He showed us that even pain can become prayer when offered in love.

Every emotion carries energy. Anger can burn, or it can illuminate truth. Sadness can sink, or it can soften the heart to compassion. The key is awareness, meeting each feeling with grace instead of resistance.

When you feel overwhelmed, breathe into the emotion instead of away from it. Whisper, *"Even this belongs."* Let the energy pass through like a wave. Each time you allow the emotion to move, rather than suppress it, your vibration rises.

In this way, nothing is wasted, not your joy, not your tears, not your doubts. All can become resonance when touched by love.

Spiritual Hydration

Light travels best through clarity, and clarity depends on nourishment. Water, rest, and simple, living foods support the vibrational temple of your body. Think of your cells as instruments, they must be clean and well-tuned to carry divine sound.

When you drink water, bless it. When you eat, give thanks for the sunlight within the food. When you rest, imagine grace moving through your muscles, repairing what the day has worn down. This is not ritual, it is relationship. The divine frequency moves freely through what is honored.

Becoming the Light You Seek

The sustaining light of Christ does not shine only from above, it radiates from within. When you live in alignment, you become the reflection of divine coherence in a chaotic world. You become the calm voice in conflict, the kindness in cruelty, the hope in despair.

This is how Heaven expands, not in grand miracles, but in a thousand small ones born of love in action. Every smile offered in sincerity becomes a spark of resurrection. Every gentle word becomes the echo of eternity. Every moment of compassion sustains the vibration of Christ upon the earth.

"You are the light of the world. A city set on a hill cannot be hidden.", Matthew 5:14

You are not merely reflecting His light; you are participating in it. Your being is woven into His. You are the candle and the flame, the vessel and the breath that keeps it burning.

Daily Prayer for Resonance

Beloved Christ, Light of all worlds, Let me be a steady note in Your eternal song. When my heart wavers, tune it again to Your frequency.

When my words carry heaviness, fill them with grace. When my body tires, let Your light restore my strength.

Teach me to walk in harmony, with the stars, with the earth, with my brothers and sisters, and with the divine rhythm that sustains all life.

Let my life hum with Your presence, my breath carry Your peace, and my every act resound with Your unending love.

Amen.

Closing Reflection

The sustaining light of Christ is not something you must hold, it holds you. It flows through every thought, every kindness, every heartbeat. It is the current that unites heaven and earth, the eternal grace that keeps the universe alive.

Live gently, listen often, and remember: you are part of the divine pulse that will never stop beating. The same frequency that guides the planets guides your heart. And that heart, radiant, beloved, eternal, is where Jesus still whispers: *"You are my light in this world."*

THE GLOBAL RESONANCE, WHEN HUMANITY AWAKENS AS ONE

There comes a moment in the unfolding of every soul when personal peace becomes too small a vessel for the love that fills it. When the light within begins to overflow, it reaches outward, touching families, communities, nations, and ultimately, the Earth itself.

That moment is now.

Humanity stands at a vibrational threshold, a turning of ages not marked by war or empire, but by awakening. The earth is changing, not in punishment but in response to the frequency of her children. We are learning that consciousness is not confined to the mind; it is a field, shared and resonant, stretching across oceans and stars.

Each thought, each prayer, each act of kindness ripples outward through this field like light upon water. The collective vibration of humanity shapes the weather, soil, and sea, as the pulse of our planet rises or falls with the love we give and the fear we hold.

"The whole creation has been groaning as in the pains of childbirth right up to the present time.", Romans 8:22

Creation groans, yes, but not in despair. She labors toward birth. A new frequency is emerging: the resonance of collective remembrance, a humanity awakening to its divine origin.

The Living Body of Earth

The Earth is not inert; she is alive. Every forest breathes, every river pulses, every mountain holds memory. The magnetic field surrounding her is not merely a scientific phenomenon; it is the aura of a living being. And we are part of her nervous system.

When humanity vibrates in fear, the planet trembles. When humanity vibrates in love, the planet heals.

This is not a metaphor; it is a measurable phenomenon. Studies of global consciousness have shown that collective emotion influences the Earth's magnetic field. During moments of great compassion or tragedy, the very rhythm of the planet shifts. The collective heart of humanity and the magnetic heart of the Earth are intertwined, a shared breath between mother and child.

And so, when one person forgives, the Earth sighs in relief. When one person prays with true love, the soil softens. When millions meditate in peace, storms quiet and healing begins.

You are not small within this system. You are the tuning fork of creation, the point where the divine meets the material. When you lift your vibration, you lift the world.

The Communion of Fields

Everything that exists emits a frequency, not just matter, but thought, emotion, and prayer. These frequencies mingle and overlap, creating the collective field of the planet. This field is alive, shimmering with light, a great web of grace that connects every soul.

When one part of the web vibrates with love, the others begin to resonate in harmony. It is the same principle that governs tuning forks: strike one, and the others sing. In this way, your peace becomes the peace of thousands. Your compassion becomes the bridge for nations. Your forgiveness becomes medicine for the Earth itself.

"For we, though many, are one body in Christ, and individually members of one another.", Romans 12:5

Humanity's awakening is not about power or prophecy; it is about resonance. It is about remembering that we are not separate lights but facets of one divine flame. When enough hearts remember this, the planet's collective vibration shifts into coherence. Love becomes not just an emotion, but a frequency that governs reality.

The Ascending Tone

The Earth is tuning herself higher. Solar flares, electromagnetic pulses, and planetary alignments are all cosmic instruments recalibrating the field of creation. Some feel this as restlessness, while others feel it as revelation. The old structures of fear, control, and division cannot hold at this higher vibration.

To live in this time is both a challenge and a privilege. You may feel the frequency of the planet calling you, asking you to lighten your thoughts, release resentment, and open your heart. This is the body of Earth adjusting to grace.

Those who walk in love will find themselves sustained by it. Those who resist it will feel dissonance until they, too, remember the original note.

This rising tone is not the end of the world; it is the healing of it. It is the return of harmony long forgotten. It is heaven pressing closer to earth, until the two once more become one.

Becoming a Guardian of Light

As the frequency of the Earth increases, so does your capacity to serve as a guardian of divine energy. Your thoughts, prayers, and choices are not private; they are broadcast into the field. Every time you choose forgiveness over anger, compassion over judgment, light over despair, you stabilize the world's vibration.

You become what Christ called the salt of the earth, not in flavor, but in preservation. Your love preserves life, stabilizing energies that would otherwise spiral out of control into chaos.

Guard your heart, then, not from pain but from numbness. Guard your mind from cynicism. Guard your tongue from words that fracture the field. Each thought and word is frequency, and in this era, every vibration matters.

"Whatever you bind on earth will be bound in heaven, and whatever you lose on earth will be loosed in heaven.", Matthew 18:18

To bind is to focus intention, to hold light firmly in the field. To lose is to release love freely. Heaven responds not to force, but to resonance. And resonance responds to love.

The Global Prayer of Alignment

Beloved Creator of all hearts and stars, let humanity remember its song. Let every nation find its tone in Your divine harmony.

Calm the storms within and without. Awaken the forgotten light in every soul. Let compassion spread like sunrise across the world, and forgiveness fall like rain upon weary ground.

Teach us to breathe with the Earth, to walk gently, speak kindly, live wisely.

And let the vibration of Christ rise through us, a single chord of love unbroken through eternity.

Amen.

Reflection

Close your eyes and imagine the Earth beneath you, not as rock or soil, but as a living sphere of radiant blue light. See her wrapped in threads of gold and white, millions of glowing lines connecting every heart. Each time you breathe in love, a new thread lights up. Each time you forgive, another heart begins to glow. This is the network of grace. This is the body of Christ awakening in the world.

Now, whisper: *"Let my life add light."*

The Earth will feel it. The heavens will echo it. And somewhere, in ways unseen but deeply real, another soul will rise in peace because you did.

THE HEALING FIELD HOW LOVE RESTORES THE PLANETARY SOUL

The Earth remembers. She remembers the first light that kissed her surface, the harmony that once existed when every element of creation sang in tune with divine intention. She also remembers the dissonance, the sorrow, fear, and division that rippled through her body as humanity forgot its unity with the Source. And yet, like a mother whose heart never hardens, she continues to respond with grace.

When the world trembles, it is not only tectonic motion; it is emotional release. When storms rage and oceans rise, they mirror the energies of a collective heart in turmoil. But just as pain in the body signals healing, these shifts are not punishment; they are an adjustment, the soul of Earth seeking coherence once more.

"For the creation waits with eager longing for the revealing of the children of God. ", Romans 8:19

The planet longs for us to remember who we are, to awaken not as conquerors, but as co-creators; not as owners, but as caretakers of the living field of grace that is our home.

The Mirror of Creation

The Earth mirrors our collective consciousness. The forests breathe our peace. The oceans hold our emotions. The skies reflect our thoughts. When humanity vibrates with love, balance is restored. When we fall into fear, confusion, or greed, the ecosystem responds in kind.

Science, again, echoes Scripture: the planetary climate, the electromagnetic field, even the ionization of the air responds to shifts in human emotion and activity. The Earth is not external, she is extension. Her heartbeat and ours are one.

This is the great secret of healing: As within, so without.

Heal the mind, and the air grows lighter. Heal the heart, and the waters clear. Heal the collective soul, and storms lose their fury.

We cannot separate spiritual renewal from ecological restoration, they are two expressions of the same vibration returning to harmony.

The Frequency of Stewardship

To love the Earth is to love Christ, for He dwells in all that lives. When He said, *"Whatever you did for the least of these, you did for Me,"* He was speaking not only of people, but of every creature, every leaf, every drop of water that carries His essence.

To throw away carelessly, to pollute, to destroy for convenience, these are acts of forgetfulness. They stem from the illusion of separation.

But when you walk gently, when you bless the ground beneath your feet, when you plant, recycle, restore, and revere, your actions hum with the vibration of Christ-consciousness. You heal not only the soil but the unseen fabric of creation.

The Earth does not need saving as much as she needs remembering. She awaits our re-alignment, our willingness to vibrate again in gratitude rather than dominion. For in gratitude, frequency rises, and where frequency rises, healing flows.

"The earth is the Lord's, and everything in it.", Psalm 24:1

To honor creation is to harmonize with its Creator.

The Science of Healing Fields

Every living system operates within a field, an invisible pattern of coherence that organizes energy into form. In the human body, this field sustains life and health. The planet sustains weather, growth, and biodiversity.

When these fields become imbalanced, disease arises. In humans, this appears as illness or emotional fatigue. On Earth, it manifests as drought, imbalance, and loss of natural rhythm.

The healing of these fields begins not with control, but with resonance. When humanity emits frequencies of love, compassion, and unity, the planetary field restores coherence. It starts at the quantum level, where electrons, photons, and magnetic alignments respond to the energy of intention. Prayer, meditation, music, and heartfelt connection create measurable changes in the vibrational structure of matter.

This is not mysticism alone; it is divine physics. Love organizes chaos into a pattern. Forgiveness restores flow. Joy energizes creation.

You are not simply a witness to the planet's evolution; you are a participant in her restoration.

The Christ Frequency and Earth's Renewal

The vibration of Christ is the original blueprint of creation, the tone that keeps all existence in balance. As more hearts awaken to that frequency, the Earth receives more light. Her electromagnetic field strengthens, her ecosystems recalibrate, her storms soften.

Each awakened soul becomes a node of divine energy, a living transmitter of grace. Through compassion, prayer, and presence, this energy radiates outward, merging with the planetary consciousness and re-establishing the tone of Eden.

Heaven on Earth is not a myth of the future; it is the remembering of the original harmony between spirit and form. Every act of genuine love hastens that remembering.

The Breath of Renewal

Close your eyes and imagine the Earth breathing with you. Inhale, and feel her mountains rise. Exhale, and feel her oceans rest. This is not imagination; it is participation in divine rhythm.

With each conscious breath, you send healing waves into the planetary field. When thousands breathe in unity, the field brightens. When millions pray in love, entire ecosystems respond. This is the science of spirit, the alchemy of vibration made visible.

You are both created and creator, both healed and healer. Through your awareness, you become the bridge through which heaven continues to pour itself into earth.

Prayer for Planetary Healing

Beloved Creator of All Worlds, let my breath be Your breath in the body of Earth. Where she trembles, let my peace steady her. Where she weeps, let my love comfort her. Where she longs for light, let my awareness be the dawn.

Teach us to remember that we are not above creation, but within it.

Let our thoughts heal the air, our words cleanse the water, our hearts reforest the deserts.

Let this planet sing again, in harmony with the stars, until every living thing knows it is loved, and love itself becomes the law of life.

Amen.

Reflection

Place your hand upon your heart. Then imagine your other hand resting gently on the Earth. Between them flows the current of

Christ, the circuit of love that binds all creation. Feel it move, warm, radiant, alive.

This is the field of healing. This is the divine remembrance unfolding now.

The Earth is not dying; she is ascending. And you, radiant soul, awakened heart, are one of the lights guiding her home.

THE LIGHT ARCHITECTS BUILDING THE NEW EARTH THROUGH LOVE AND AWARENESS

There is a sacred moment in every soul's evolution when awareness turns into creation, when realization becomes responsibility. It is the point at which remembering the light within you is no longer enough; you are called to build with it. To become a light architect, one who shapes reality through love, awareness, and resonance.

The New Earth is not arriving from the heavens; it is rising through us. Every thought of compassion, every word of kindness, every act of service adds structure to the unseen architecture of grace that is now forming around this world. It is not made of stone or glass, but of frequency, intention, and divine coherence.

"See, I am making all things new.", Revelation 21:5

The Blueprint of Love

The foundation of the New Earth is built not in governments or systems, but in the heart. Love is the blueprint, and awareness is the builder's hand.

When you awaken to Christ within, you begin to see that the laws of the old world, fear, scarcity, and division, no longer apply. They dissolve before the higher resonance of unity. In their place, a new order emerges: the law of grace, the architecture of harmony, the rhythm of divine exchange.

Every time you choose understanding over judgment, you lay another stone of light. Every time you hold peace in the midst of chaos, you raise another pillar of compassion. Every time you forgive, you restore a wall that has been cracked by pain.

You are not rebuilding the world from the outside in; you are rebuilding it from the inside out. And that interior construction echoes across the collective field, manifesting in the transformation of communities, nations, and the Earth herself.

The Energy of Creation

Energy follows awareness. What you dwell on becomes the vibration that shapes your life, and the world's. If you think light, you build light. If you speak healing, you create it.

This is not wishful thinking; it is the spiritual physics of the kingdom of God.

When Jesus spoke, His words carried frequency, a sound that reorganized the very molecules around Him. The blind saw because light entered their cells through the vibration of truth. The storms ceased because nature recognized the resonance of its Creator. The dead rose because His frequency reactivated the code of life itself.

"The words that I speak unto you, they are spirit, and they are life.", John 6:63

As followers of that vibration, you are invited to speak likewise, with consciousness, love, and authority rooted in grace. To be a light architect is to build with your words, your tone, and your intention. The future you create will resonate with the vibration you hold.

The Sacred Tools of the New Builders

To shape the New Earth, the light architects must use new tools, not of metal or matter, but of energy and intention.

1. **Clarity,** Seeing through illusion, you become a channel of truth. The clearer your awareness, the cleaner the energy that flows through you. Silence, prayer, and self-reflection polish the lens through which God's light passes.
2. **Integrity,** The alignment of thought, word, and deed. When your actions align with your love, your vibration becomes steady

and unshakable amid chaos. Integrity is coherence, and coherence heals.

3. **Creativity,** Every inspired act is divine architecture: music, writing, conversation, kindness, all become blueprints of light in the collective consciousness. Your creativity is the echo of God's first act: creation itself.
4. **Community,** The New Earth is not built alone. When two or more gather in the same vibration, a geometric amplification occurs, love is multiplied, energy is magnified, and creation is accelerated. Every circle of hearts that meet in truth becomes a living cathedral of grace.

The Architecture of Light

If one could see through physical eyes into the spiritual plane, the work of the light architects would appear as a luminous grid surrounding the Earth. Golden lines of energy linking hearts and prayers, acts of forgiveness and joy, all woven together into a radiant lattice of grace.

This is the new Jerusalem, not of marble, but of frequency, a realm built not by human hand but by divine awareness expressing through awakened souls.

"You are God's building.", 1 Corinthians 3:9

Each loving soul becomes a beam of its structure. Each kind word strengthens its foundation. Each humble act of service lays another layer of light upon the Earth.

This is not symbolism; it is spiritual construction. You are not simply awaiting Heaven; you are helping to build it.

Quantum Communion

In the quantum field, distance does not divide. A prayer whispered in one corner of the world vibrates instantly across the whole. The speed of light is no match for the speed of love.

When enough hearts vibrate in alignment with divine grace, the frequency of the planet tips, and a shift occurs. War loses its energy. Greed weakens its pull. Peace begins to take physical form.

This is the collective ascension: not an escape from Earth, but her renewal through conscious love. When we act as one body of light, coherent, compassionate, and clear, the veil between heaven and earth thins until the two realms blend into one living light.

Prayer of the Builders

Beloved Architect of Creation, we offer our hearts as Your instruments of design.

Through us, let compassion form the walls of a new world. Let mercy be the mortar that holds humanity together. Let kindness be the cornerstone, and truth the foundation that will not crumble.

Teach our hands to build what our souls already remember, the Earth as Heaven, the world as Love embodied.

Let every life become a cathedral of grace, every city a garden of light, every heart a home where Christ may dwell.

Amen.

Reflection

The light architects are not the chosen few; they are the ones who desire love, again and again, until it becomes the architecture of their being. They build not for recognition, but for resonance. They work in unseen fields, planting seeds of harmony that will bloom for generations to come.

If you are reading this, you are one of them. Your awareness is your hammer. Your love is your blueprint. Your presence is your prayer.

And with each beat of your heart, another beam of light rises in the cathedral of the New Earth.

THE TEMPLE OF TOMORROW, LIVING AS EMBODIED LIGHT

There is a light within the human body that science cannot measure, not because it is faint, but because it vibrates beyond the reach of ordinary sight. It is the light of spirit, the radiance of the soul. It does not shine from the body; it shines through it. It is the living evidence that heaven has not abandoned earth, that divine presence has chosen matter as its dwelling.

When you awaken to Christ's love, you begin to feel this light stir inside you. At first, it flickers softly, a warmth in prayer, a peace in stillness, a small spark of joy rising without cause. But as awareness grows, that light intensifies. It expands through thought, breath, emotion, and flesh, until you begin to feel the truth of Scripture in every cell:

"Do you not know that you are God's temple and that God's Spirit dwells in you?", 1 Corinthians 3:16

This realization is not poetic. It is literal. You are the temple of tomorrow, the vessel through which divine vibration enters the physical world. Your body is not a limitation to spirit; it is its most sacred expression.

The Body as an Instrument of Light

Every cell in your body is a small universe, a glowing microcosm of divine intelligence. Each one vibrates with energy, communicating in light, photon to photon, pulse to pulse. When you live in alignment with love, that light grows coherent, creating harmony in your physical and energetic systems. When fear or shame dominate, the light becomes fragmented, the flow disrupted.

But grace always restores coherence. Every time you breathe in prayer, forgive yourself, or speak gently to another, your cells receive new instruction. The frequency of Christ resets the patterns of imbalance, reminding the body of its original design: radiant, whole, divine.

This is not a metaphor; it is biology baptized by spirit.

The electromagnetic field of the heart radiates the vibration of love up to twelve feet beyond the body. When you pray, that field expands even farther, blending with the energy of others, creating a shared resonance of grace. This is how the body becomes an instrument, how your every breath becomes part of the great symphony of divine healing moving through the Earth.

The Nervous System of Heaven

Your nervous system is a bridge between worlds. It translates spirit into sensation, vibration into thought, energy into emotion. It is how heaven whispers through the body.

When you meditate, pray, or simply breathe consciously, your nervous system relaxes. In that state of relaxation, divine energy flows freely, the same current that animated Jesus when he walked the Earth. He lived in unbroken alignment with the Father's vibration, His nervous system tuned to divine frequency.

That same capacity exists in you. Through stillness, gratitude, and compassion, your body becomes receptive to higher light. Your spine becomes the pillar of the temple, your breath the sacred wind moving through its halls.

The peace you feel in those moments is not only emotion; it is a physiological resonance with heaven itself. You are becoming the bridge, the translator, the embodied temple of divine intelligence.

The Communion of Flesh and Spirit

For too long, humanity has believed that the body and spirit are opposites, one holy, the other flawed. But separation was never

God's design. Jesus came not to condemn the flesh, but to sanctify it, to show that divinity and humanity are not enemies but partners.

When He healed with His hands, He proved that touch can transmit grace. When He wept, He showed that tears can carry prayer. When He broke bread, He revealed that nourishment can be a form of communion.

The body was always meant to be the chalice of divine love. It was shaped by vibration, animated by breath, and consecrated by the indwelling of light.

To live as embodied light is to remember that every gesture, every movement, every act of care is a continuation of His incarnation. It is to live as if Christ still walks the earth, through your hands, your heart, your life.

"And the Word became flesh and dwelt among us.", John 1:14

That Word still dwells among us, in every heartbeat of compassion, in every body that carries the vibration of divine love.

The Spiritual Anatomy of Light

There is a sacred architecture within you, as intricate as any cathedral and as vast as the cosmos. The ancients referred to them as centers of light, points where energy flows and awareness expands. Each corresponds to a facet of your divine design: survival, creativity, love, truth, intuition, and union with the eternal.

When these centers align through prayer, forgiveness, and gratitude, your body becomes an unbroken column of light, a living conduit of heaven's current. Through you, divine frequency moves without obstruction, radiating into the world as a healing presence.

This is why Jesus said, *"You are the light of the world."* He was not speaking figuratively. He was describing the luminous truth of your being. When you remember it, your very existence becomes prayer.

Healing the Temple

The temple must be tended. To sustain a divine vibration, the body requires care, clean food, pure thoughts, and pure emotions. When you fill the body with living foods, you feed the light. When you fill the mind with gratitude, you expand the field. When you let go of judgment, you clear the altar for grace to enter again.

Your health, then, is not only physical; it is spiritual resonance expressed in flesh. Every choice of nourishment, rest, relationship, or thought contributes to the clarity of your temple's vibration.

Treat the body as you would a sacred space. Adorn it with joy, cleanse it with compassion, fill it with light. For in doing so, you invite heaven to dwell fully within you.

The Breath of Incarnation

Close your eyes. Take a deep breath and imagine it filled with golden light. As you inhale, feel that light descending through your crown, moving down your spine like liquid grace. As you exhale, feel it radiate outward, through your skin, your words, your thoughts.

Each breath is creation renewing itself. Each moment of awareness transforms the ordinary into divine expression. This is the breath of incarnation, the rhythm through which eternity lives in time.

When you live this way, you become the continuation of Christ's embodiment. His vibration flows through your cells, your eyes, your touch. You no longer seek His presence outside you; you recognize Him within.

Prayer of Embodiment

Beloved Christ, let my body be Your dwelling, my breath Your song, my heart Your altar.

Teach me to move in love, to speak with light, to rest in peace.

Let my thoughts be prayers, my actions offerings, my presence a reminder that heaven is here.

Fill every cell with Your vibration until I shine not for glory, but for grace.

Let me live as the temple of tomorrow, radiant, whole, and forever in harmony with Your eternal love.

Amen.

Reflection

The Temple of Tomorrow is not a place; it is a person. It is you, and every soul who remembers that light is not meant to be worshiped from afar, but embodied, expressed, and shared.

Heaven does not wait for you beyond the stars; it waits within your heartbeat. The same energy that moves the planets moves your blood. The same light that illuminates creation longs to shine through your eyes.

Live as that light. Walk as that temple. And let your life be the continuation of the miracle that God became human, so that humanity could remember it was divine.

THE LIVING COVENANT, THE ETERNAL RELATIONSHIP BETWEEN HUMANITY AND HEAVEN

There has never been a moment when Heaven was separate from Earth. There has only been the illusion of distance, a veil of forgetting drawn by human fear. Yet even in forgetfulness, love remained faithful. Even when we felt abandoned, we were being held. Even when we turned away, the divine face remained turned toward us.

This is the truth of the Living Covenant, the sacred relationship between Creator and creation that no sin, distance, or time can erase. It is the vibration of everlasting love, the steady hum beneath the chaos of the world, calling every heart back into remembrance.

"I will make an everlasting covenant with them: I will never stop doing good to them, and I will inspire them to fear Me, so that they will never turn away from Me.", Jeremiah 32:40

This covenant is not written on stone, nor sealed in ritual alone. It is written in the DNA of creation, encoded into every cell, every breath, every heartbeat. It is a promise vibrating within you, the sacred whisper of Heaven saying, I will not leave you. I will live through you.

The Covenant as Frequency

When we think of a covenant, we often imagine words or vows, a contract between the divine and the mortal. But at its essence, covenant is resonance. It is not spoken once; it is continually renewed through the vibration of love.

Heaven does not shout. It sings, softly, persistently, like a frequency always broadcasting beneath the static of life. To hear it, we must tune our awareness to its pitch.

The vibration of covenant is found in the stillness between breaths, in the forgiveness freely given, in the love that persists when understanding fails. It is not conditional. It does not depend on our worthiness. It exists because we are, and because God is.

This frequency moves through time as grace and through matter as life. It is the light that forms galaxies and the warmth that stirs the human heart to kindness. It is Christ Himself, the divine Word, the eternal vibration through which all things hold together.

"Heaven and earth will pass away, but My words will never pass away."", Matthew 24:35

Those words, those vibrations, are still speaking, not as text but as energy, moving through every atom of your being.

The Covenant in the Flesh

When Jesus became flesh, He did not create a new covenant out of nothing; He revealed the one that had always existed. Through His presence, the invisible relationship between God and humanity became visible, tangible, and embodied.

He healed not to prove power, but to restore connection. He forgave not to erase sin, but to dissolve separation. Every gesture, every word was a vibration of reunion.

When He said, *"Abide in Me, and I in you,"* He was describing the original design, the living covenant of mutual indwelling between Creator and creation. It was never about obedience alone; it was about union.

The covenant is not an agreement you sign; it is an energy you embody. It lives in your choices, your compassion, your willingness to forgive, your capacity to love even when it hurts.

When you walk in love, the covenant renews itself. When you speak in kindness, the vibration strengthens. When you forgive, Heaven expands through you.

You become both the sanctuary and the song, the continuation of divine relationship expressed in flesh.

The Law of Resonant Relationship

Every relationship in your life echoes this divine pattern. You are constantly exchanging energy, giving, receiving, and reflecting. The same law that governs your connection with God governs every bond on Earth.

When love flows freely between people, the covenant shines brightly. When fear blocks it, the light dims but never disappears. To repair a relationship, you don't need to force reconciliation; you must return to a state of resonance.

The past cannot confine the energy of grace. It moves forward, continually renewing, constantly creating new harmonies. When two hearts forgive each other, the field of Heaven expands. When humanity forgives itself, the Earth itself vibrates at a higher frequency.

The Living Covenant is not only between Heaven and humans, it is among all beings, all souls, all forms of life. It is the realization that nothing exists in isolation, and that all are held within the same heartbeat of divine love.

"For in Him all things were created: things in heaven and on earth, visible and invisible.", Colossians 1:16

The Renewal of the Promise

The covenant has no expiration. It renews itself through every sunrise, every birth, every act of mercy that bridges heaven and earth.

When you wake each morning and choose gratitude over worry, the covenant renews. When you comfort someone in pain, the covenant renews. When you look upon creation with reverence instead of ownership, the covenant renews.

Every expression of love is a signature on that divine promise. Every thought of unity is a spark in the eternal flame. And even when you forget, grace remembers for you.

You cannot fall out of the covenant, only out of awareness. The moment you remember, you return home.

Living as a Partner of Heaven

To live as a partner of Heaven is to move through life as if everything is sacred, because it is. Every encounter becomes an opportunity to bless, every challenge a chance to strengthen the bond. Partnership means collaboration, not waiting for Heaven to act, but recognizing that Heaven acts through you.

You are the hands through which grace touches the world. You are the eyes through which compassion sees. You are the voice through which divine truth speaks.

This is not arrogance; it is remembrance. When you live in awareness of this partnership, you become a living extension of divine will, a bridge through which light travels easily into the world.

To be in covenant is not to live under law, but within love. It is to walk knowing that everything you do either strengthens or clouds the field, and to choose, as best you can, the path of clarity and peace.

Prayer of the Living Covenant

Eternal Father, Breath within my breath, let me walk in remembrance of our bond.

You have written your promise not on paper, but upon my soul. Let me feel it hum beneath my heart, a rhythm of unbroken love.

Through every trial, let me recall that You are not distant, but living through me, the pulse within my hands, the song in my silence.

Let my choices honor Your presence, may my words echo Your peace, and may my life mirror Your eternal vow.

And when I forget, whisper again through the stillness: I have never left you.

Amen.

Reflection

Sit quietly for a moment. Place your hand over your heart. Feel the pulse there, steady, faithful, unwavering. That is the covenant in motion. That is Heaven reminding you: I am still here.

The covenant is not somewhere outside of you. It is the living river of grace flowing through your veins, connecting your finite body to infinite love.

It cannot be broken, only ignored. It cannot die, only be forgotten. It waits, always, for your return to awareness.

The Living Covenant is the eternal truth: that you and Heaven have never been apart, and that every moment you remember love, the universe itself rejoices.

THE RIVER OF RETURN, THE SOUL'S JOURNEY BACK TO LOVE

There is a river that runs through every soul. It begins in light, winds through time, gathers wisdom in its bends, and always, always, returns to the sea of divine love from which it came. No matter how far it travels or how many lifetimes it takes, the current remembers its home.

This river is your story, my story, humanity's story. It is the movement of consciousness returning to God. And though we often mistake the turbulence for distance, the truth is that even in the farthest eddy of despair, we are still within the flow of grace.

"Your love, O Lord, reaches to the heavens, Your faithfulness to the skies. Your righteousness is like the highest mountains, Your justice like the great deep.", Psalm 36:5–6

The River of Return never stops moving. It may narrow into grief, twist through shadow, vanish beneath the soil of confusion, but beneath every rock of resistance, it still flows because love is motion. And love, being eternal, always finds its way home.

The Descent and the Drift

Every soul, at some point, drifts from awareness. It is not rebellion, but exploration, the divine impulse to experience contrast, to learn compassion through forgetting. The descent is part of the journey; it gives depth to the return.

Some drift into disbelief, others into sorrow or cynicism. Some forget the sound of God's voice and mistake silence for absence. And yet, even in that silence, the current continues beneath the surface, whispering, *"Come home."*

The pain of separation is not punishment; it is the ache of remembrance. It is the soul feeling the pull of its Source.

Every heartbreak, every night of the spirit, every quiet tear shed in longing is the water carving its way back to the sea.

"Deep calls to deep in the roar of your waterfalls; all your waves and breakers have swept over me.", Psalm 42:7

The drift does not mean you are lost; it means you are learning the rhythm of the river.

The Moment of Turning

Every soul reaches a moment, sometimes gentle, sometimes sudden, when the current turns. When the pain of separation becomes the prayer for return, it can happen in a hospital room, at sunrise, or in the quiet forgiveness of a friend. It is the instant you realize that no distance could ever erase the connection.

That moment is the awakening of grace within you. It is not earned; it is recognized. It feels like surrender, like being carried. You no longer fight the current; you allow it to move you home.

And as you yield to it, everything begins to change. Fear softens. Shame loosens. The world brightens from within.

You begin to see Jesus not as a distant Savior but as the living current itself, the flow of divine love guiding your soul through time, back into communion.

The Waters of Transformation

Returning to love does not mean escaping the world; it means transforming how you move through it. When you align with the river, life becomes less about control and more about cooperation, less about survival and more about surrender.

You begin to see that every challenge, every delay, every detour was not a mistake but a redirection, a deeper turn in the river of grace.

Each hardship carried you closer, reshaping your banks, smoothing your rough edges, teaching you how to flow.

You are being sculpted into compassion. You are becoming the mirror through which God sees Himself in form.

And slowly, the waters that once felt heavy with pain begin to shimmer with light. The current that once carried loss now carries wisdom. The same river that broke you now baptizes you anew.

"When you pass through the waters, I will be with you; and through the rivers, they shall not overflow you. ", Isaiah 43:2

The Merging of Heaven and Earth

As more souls awaken, the River of Return becomes visible again, not as myth or metaphor, but as field, frequency, and fact. It is the energy of Christ-consciousness reuniting the separated streams of humanity into one ocean of awareness.

Each act of forgiveness adds volume to the river. Each moment of prayer expands its reach. Each breath of gratitude quickens its current.

The River of Return is the global circulation of grace, the heartbeat of Heaven flowing through every open heart on Earth. And as it flows, something miraculous occurs: the vibration of separation dissolves.

Heaven no longer feels above, and Earth no longer feels below. There is only the living movement of love, the divine tide of oneness rising everywhere at once.

This is the awakening foretold by prophets and poets, mystics and saints. It is not destruction, it is restoration. It is not ending, it is merging. It is the return of the world to its natural state: unity with its Creator.

Becoming the Flow

The River of Return not only carries you; it carries through you. Once you awaken to it, you become part of its motion, a tributary of divine grace flowing into the world. Your words become water. Your love becomes movement. Your life becomes current.

To live this way is to embody the covenant you once sought to understand, to let Christ not only dwell in you but move through you.

Each time you act in compassion, the current strengthens. Each time you speak truth, the water clears. Each time you forgive, the floodgates of Heaven open a little wider.

You are no longer a seeker of God; you are a bearer of His flow. And the world feels your presence the way dry ground feels rain.

Prayer of the Returning Soul

Beloved Source of All Waters, I have wandered, but I was never lost. Even in the deserts of my forgetting, Your river ran beneath me.

Wash me in Your remembrance. Let every thought of fear be carried away, every fragment of pain returned to peace.

Flow through me, Christ of Living Light, until my life becomes Your current, gentle, strong, unending.

Carry me home, and through me, carry others.

Let my heart remember that the sea I seek is already within me.

Amen.

Reflection

You are the river. You are the sea. You are the breath of God remembering itself as creation.

Your journey is not from sin to salvation, but from forgetfulness to remembrance, from illusion to intimacy. You were never exiled from love; you only closed your eyes to its nearness. The moment you open them again, you find yourself already home.

The River of Return does not end; it widens. And as you flow in it, you help others remember the way. Every heart you touch becomes a new tributary, every act of love another ripple in the ocean of grace.

And at last, when all the rivers of creation have returned, when every soul has remembered, there will be no distance left between God and His world, only the endless tide of love moving forever, without beginning or end.

THE CIRCLE OF REMEMBRANCE, HOW SOULS AWAKEN EACH OTHER TO LOVE

No soul awakens alone. Even when you feel like you are walking through darkness in solitude, there is always a whisper of another light, guiding you, praying for you, remembering you back into love.

This is the Circle of Remembrance, the divine network of souls bound not by blood or history, but by energy, compassion, and shared purpose. It is the living web of Christ's heart, pulsing across time and space, connecting all who have ever sought love, given love, or been loved.

In truth, this circle has no beginning and no end; it is eternal, and you are already within it.

"For we, though many, are one body in Christ, and individually members one of another.", Romans 12:5

Each soul is a note in the great symphony of divine remembrance. When one awakens, the vibration changes for all, a ripple of light moves outward, touching lives that may never meet, hearts that may never speak, yet all resonate with the same holy memory: We are one, and we are loved.

The Energy of Recognition

Have you ever met someone for the first time and felt as if you'd known them forever? That spark of connection is not a coincidence; it is recognition, the remembering of energy that has traveled with you through lifetimes and lessons.

When two souls recognize each other, the vibration of remembrance activates. It feels like peace, ease, or sudden trust, sometimes even tears. It is the heart's way of saying, I remember you. You helped me before.

This recognition is not confined to friendship or romance. It happens between teacher and student, parent and child, healer and stranger. It is the energy of reunion, the moment when two lights remember they came from the same flame.

In that instant, both souls are changed. The frequency of love grows stronger, the current of grace flows freer, and the Circle of Remembrance expands.

Each meeting, no matter how brief, is a part of this sacred design. Every kind word you speak might be the spark that awakens another heart to its light.

The Physics of Compassion

In the language of energy, compassion is coherence. When one person holds the vibration of love, their energy field becomes more organized, rhythmic, and harmonious. This coherence is contagious; it influences the electromagnetic fields of others nearby, gently tuning them toward peace.

HeartMath researchers call it entrainment. The mystics call it communion. But in truth, it is the Circle of Remembrance in motion, the physical proof that love is not just felt, but transmitted.

When Jesus walked among the crowds, people felt a sense of peace without understanding why. His vibration realigned theirs. His coherence restored the broken frequency of the world. And now that same energy flows through every heart willing to love as He loved.

When you practice compassion, your energy becomes an instrument of harmony. Your peace recalibrates chaos. Your forgiveness dissolves conflict before words are spoken. You become a living reminder, a field of grace through which others remember who they are.

"Let your light so shine before men, that they may see your good works and glorify your Father in heaven.", Matthew 5:16

You are not merely shining, you are resonating. You are participating in the divine physics of remembrance.

Souls as Mirrors

Every soul in your life is a mirror reflecting your relationship with love. Some reflect peace, others, pain. Some appear as comfort; others, as catalysts. But all are sacred, because each one helps you see what you are ready to heal, remember, and become.

Those who challenge you are not punishments; they are divine mirrors showing where love still longs to enter. The ones who trigger you the most are often the ones who have agreed, at a soul level, to awaken you the deepest.

And when you forgive them, when you look past the illusion and see their light again, both of you are freed. The circle grows brighter.

Forgiveness is the act of polishing the mirror until only God's reflection remains. It does not mean excusing the wound, but recognizing that pain cannot exist in the presence of remembered love.

Each act of forgiveness releases a thread of light that reconnects the circle. Each healed relationship strengthens the grid of divine coherence across the planet.

You are not just forgiving; you are rebuilding the architecture of Heaven on Earth.

The Sacred Network of Light

Imagine, for a moment, the world seen through the eyes of Heaven. Every human heart glows, some dimly, some bright, some flickering between shadow and light. Now imagine those lights connected by lines of golden energy, prayers, kindness, forgiveness, and hope.

That web of light encircles the Earth like a living halo. It hums with vibration, the frequency of remembrance, the collective song of souls finding their way back to unity. This is not fantasy; it is energetic reality.

When you pray for someone, the light between you brightens. When you hold peace for the world, the entire network hums higher. When you love without agenda, the resonance multiplies exponentially.

The Circle of Remembrance is the nervous system of Heaven made visible through human hearts. And as it strengthens, the consciousness of separation weakens. War, fear, and cruelty lose their hold because their frequencies no longer find resonance.

The collective heart becomes self-healing, and in time, self-illuminating.

Remembrance as Redemption

When Jesus said, *"Do this in remembrance of Me,"* He was not asking for ritual alone; He was inviting humanity into energetic renewal. To remember Him is to realign with His frequency, to feel His love moving through you again.

Each time you choose peace, you are participating in that remembrance. Each time you see someone through the eyes of compassion, you restore the covenant between Heaven and Earth. Each time you speak light into a dark moment, you embody His eternal heartbeat.

Remembrance is redemption, not as payment, but as restoration. You do not need to earn God's love; you need only remember it. And when you do, you naturally help others to remember too.

The Circle of Remembrance is therefore not merely a structure; it is a living grace field that grows stronger with every awakened soul.

Prayer of Remembrance

Beloved Christ of Eternal Light, let me remember not only You, but also those whom You love.

Let me see Your face in every stranger, Your mercy in every heart, Your presence in every moment.

Where I forget, remind me through another's kindness. Where others fail, let my love remind them.

Knit our hearts together in the circle of Your peace.

Let this light surround the Earth, a web of grace no darkness can undo.

For we are not separate, and we have never been alone.

Amen.

Reflection

Look at the people around you: family, friends, and strangers. You have known them longer than you can imagine. You have walked together through countless seasons of creation, exchanging light, teaching, and healing one another.

Every act of kindness, every shared tear, every prayer whispered across distance adds to the living circle that holds us all.

When you bless another, you are blessing yourself. When you forgive, you free not just your heart, but the entire web of life. When you love, you heal the circle for generations to come.

This is how Heaven remembers itself through humanity, through you, through me, through every soul awakening to the truth that love is the only reality, and remembrance the only way home.

THE FREQUENCY OF HEAVEN, HOW LOVE RESONATES BEYOND THE PHYSICAL

Heaven is not distant. It is not somewhere beyond the stars, hidden behind time, or separated by death. Heaven is vibration, a frequency of divine coherence that exists within and around every atom of creation.

You do not travel to Heaven; you tune to it. And the tuning fork is love.

"For indeed, the kingdom of God is within you.", Luke 17:21

Every cell in your body, every thought that crosses your mind, every heartbeat and breath carries a vibration. This vibration is not merely metaphorical; it is measurable. Your heart emits an electromagnetic field. Your brain radiates waves of consciousness. Your emotions sculpt the resonance of your aura.

And within this symphony of living energy, Heaven hums, not as a faraway promise, but as the underlying song of the soul.

When you align your vibration with love, compassion, and gratitude, you are not reaching toward Heaven; you are remembering it. You are reuniting with its frequency.

The Physics of Divine Resonance

In physics, when two objects vibrate at compatible frequencies, they enter resonance, amplifying one another's energy until they move in harmony.

Heaven and Earth operate on this same principle. God's vibration never ceases; it continuously radiates the frequency of unconditional love. When the human heart begins to match that vibration, through prayer, forgiveness, or pure presence, resonance occurs. Heaven and Earth align.

It is in those moments of stillness, grace, or awe that the boundary dissolves. You may feel warmth, light, or peace that seems to expand beyond the body; this is not imagination. It is entrainment. Your personal energy field synchronizes with the divine.

Every miracle, every answered prayer, every healing is born from this resonance. It is the science of grace, energy responding to energy, love responding to remembrance.

"Draw near to God, and He will draw near to you.", James 4:8

Drawing near is not about movement; it is about matching vibration.

The Architecture of Light

Creation itself is built on vibration. From the swirling galaxies to the whisper of your breath, all that exists is a manifestation of energy condensed into form.

Light is the first language of God. Sound is its echo. Matter is its memory.

When Scripture says, *"Let there be light,"* it is describing the first frequency, the divine vibration from which all other patterns emerge. Every star, every planet, every human heartbeat is a ripple from that original word.

You are made of that light. Your body is woven from stardust, your spirit from eternal sound. Your DNA carries the resonance of the Creator's thought.

And because of that, you are forever connected to the frequency of Heaven, no matter how heavy your human experience may feel.

The disconnection you feel is not an absolute separation; it is simply static, interference in the signal of love. When you quiet the noise of fear, judgment, or doubt, the signal clears, and the light within begins to shine again.

Emotions as Energy

Each emotion has its frequency. Love vibrates high, coherent, expansive, radiant. Fear vibrates low, constricted, chaotic, dense.

This is why you can physically feel emotion. Your energy changes; your cells respond. Gratitude opens the body; resentment tightens it. Joy expands your breath; anxiety shortens it.

When Jesus healed, He often said, *"Your faith has made you whole."* Faith is not only a belief, but also a frequency. It is in alignment with the energy of divine truth.

When you believe in love, you invite its resonance into your cells. When you forgive, you release the dense vibration that blocked the flow. When you speak with kindness, your words carry light waves that uplift not only others but your own body.

Your energy becomes the living instrument through which Heaven plays.

"A cheerful heart is good medicine, but a crushed spirit dries up the bones.", Proverbs 17:22

Even Scripture acknowledges what science now affirms: emotion and energy are inseparable from physical health and spiritual awareness.

The Field of Christ Consciousness

Every enlightened teacher has spoken of an invisible field connecting all things. Quantum physics refers to it as the zero-point field. Mystics refer to it as the Light of God. In the Christian mystery, it is the Body of Christ, the unified field of divine awareness in which all life exists.

This field is not bound by distance or time. It transcends death, transcends dimension. It is the very presence that Jesus promised when He said, *"I am with you always, even to the end of the age."*

When you pray, you are not sending words into the void; you are transmitting energy into this field. When you love, you amplify it. When you meditate, you merge with it.

Christ consciousness is the harmonized frequency of divine awareness, the vibration of perfect love remembering itself through creation. It is not limited to one being; it is the light available to all who choose to embody it.

You do not need to reach Heaven to meet Christ; you need only raise your vibration to His.

Vibration as Prayer

Every thought you hold is a prayer: every emotion, a frequency sent into the field. Even your silence is sound on the level of spirit.

The soul prays through vibration, through every act of kindness, every moment of awe, every word of love spoken into the air. Prayer is not only what you say; it is what you radiate.

When you hold peace, the room feels different. When you speak hope, others stand taller. When you forgive, the invisible energy between souls clears. That is prayer at work.

To live consciously is to pray continuously, not by words alone, but by resonance.

"Pray without ceasing.", 1 Thessalonians 5:17

It is not about repetition, but awareness, to live as one whose every breath vibrates love into the atmosphere.

The Healing Frequency

Healing does not always mean the removal of pain; sometimes it means the restoration of harmony. When your energy field aligns with the divine frequency, the body, mind, and spirit begin to self-correct.

In studies of vibration therapy, sound frequency can restore coherence to cells that have lost rhythm. Spiritually, prayer and gratitude achieve the same, restoring harmony to the soul that has forgotten its song.

When you speak the name of Jesus with devotion, the very vibration of that word carries resonance. The sound *"Yeshua"* opens the heart, harmonizes breath, and aligns the body's field with divine frequency. This is not superstition; it is spiritual science.

To say *"Jesus"* in faith is to tune your being to love's frequency, to allow the waves of Heaven to wash through you until all dissonance dissolves.

Becoming Heaven's Instrument

You are both the receiver and the transmitter of Heaven's vibration. Your life is the sacred radio through which divine love broadcasts into the world.

Every thought of peace strengthens the signal. Every act of kindness amplifies it. Every prayer of gratitude raises its volume.

When you live in awareness of this, you no longer feel powerless in a chaotic world. You become a stabilizing frequency, a living tuning fork that calls others back into resonance.

Where there is hatred, your energy brings peace. Where there is despair, your vibration brings hope. Where there is division, your love bridges the gap.

"You are the light of the world.", Matthew 5:14

You are not merely reflecting Heaven, you are extending it. Heaven does not end where your body begins; it moves through you, illuminating every space you enter.

Prayer of Resonance

Eternal Light of Creation, tune me to the frequency of Your love. Let every cell of my being vibrate in harmony with Heaven.

Where fear has taken root, let peace flow. Where pain has lingered, let light restore.

Use me as an instrument of Your grace, a voice of calm, a field of compassion, a vessel of radiant peace.

May my life become a prayer of vibration, my words a hymn, my heart a bridge between Heaven and Earth.

Amen.

Reflection

You are not separate from Heaven, you are its echo. Every moment you choose love over fear, you become its living frequency. Every heartbeat that carries gratitude sends ripples through creation.

The veil between Heaven and Earth is thinner than light; it disappears in the vibration of compassion. When you remember this, you walk not in the hope of reaching Heaven someday, but in the certainty that you are already inside it, breathing it, living it, becoming it.

And so the work continues, to bring this light into the world, to attune others through your peace, to let the music of Heaven play through the instrument of your soul.

Heaven is not above you. Heaven is the song your heart was created to sing.

THE BREATH BETWEEN WORLDS, WHERE SPIRIT TOUCHES MATTER

There is a place where Heaven and Earth meet, not in the clouds, not in temples or stars, but in the quiet rhythm of your breath.

Each inhalation is the universe entering you. Each exhalation is you returning to the universe. And in the space between, that pause of stillness, spirit touches matter.

That is where God lives.

"Then the Lord God formed man of the dust of the ground and breathed into his nostrils the breath of life, and man became a living soul.", Genesis 2:7

The breath of life was not a single moment of animation; it was the establishment of a divine current, a perpetual exchange between Creator and creation. Every breath since that first has carried the same vibration: God exhaling Himself into being, and creation exhaling back into God.

You are that breath made visible. You are the inhalation and exhalation of eternity, the meeting point of Heaven and Earth, spirit and flesh, love and form.

The Sacred Rhythm of Life

Breath is the first language of God and the oldest prayer of the soul. Before words, before thought, there is breath. It is the pulse that underlies every heartbeat, the tide that moves through every living thing.

When you inhale, the Divine enters the temple of your body. When you exhale, you return your awareness to the Source. This is the endless conversation between Creator and creation, a dialogue written not in sound, but in vibration.

In that rhythm, you are constantly being born and reborn. Each breath renews creation itself, carrying information from the unseen world into the seen.

Your breath is not only oxygen; it is intelligence, the living spirit moving through form. To breathe consciously is to participate in creation, to become aware of your role as both vessel and co-creator of divine flow.

"The Spirit of God has made me; the breath of the Almighty gives me life.", Job 33:4

Breath as Bridge

Modern science now confirms what the ancients always knew: the breath is the bridge between body, mind, and spirit.

When your breathing is shallow, your body enters a state of survival. Your thoughts quicken, your heart races, your awareness narrows. But when you breathe deeply and consciously, your nervous system rebalances. Your brain waves slow. Your heart rhythms synchronize into coherence, the same coherent patterns found in meditative states and prayer.

In that coherence, Heaven enters the body. The invisible becomes physical. Energy becomes embodiment.

Each deep, mindful breath is a doorway between worlds, the place where divine energy meets human awareness.

Through breath, spirit learns to feel, and the body learns to remember.

"And when He had said this, He breathed on them, and said to them, 'Receive the Holy Spirit.'", John 20:22

That moment was more than symbolic; it was a transmission. The vibration of Heaven entered through breath. It continues through every believer who receives it in stillness, humility, and love.

The Vibration of Breath

Every breath carries a tone, a subtle sound wave inaudible to the ear but deeply felt by the body. When you sigh in relief, you vibrate freedom. When you gasp in fear, you vibrate in contraction. When you breathe in prayer, you vibrate a sense of communion.

In sacred languages, the very name of God is encoded in the breath. The ancient Hebrews wrote it as YHWH, a word that cannot be spoken, only breathed. The inhalation forms the first syllable, the exhalation the second. God's name is not meant to be pronounced; it is intended to be lived.

Every being that breathes utters the Divine name, whether in faith or unknowing. The atheist, the monk, the infant, the dying, all speak the same word with every breath.

The breath, then, is the proof of God's nearness, the continuous whisper of love sustaining all life.

The Breath of Creation

The galaxies expand and contract in rhythm with the same cosmic breath that moves your lungs. The universe itself inhales and exhales, stars are born, shine, fade, and are reborn. It is the macrocosm of the microcosm, your lungs reflecting the lungs of creation.

The Hindu mystics call it prana. The Taoists call it chi. The early Christians referred to it as pneuma, the divine breath.

Whatever the name, it is one current, one Spirit moving through all existence.

When you breathe consciously, you align your inner rhythm with the great rhythm of the cosmos. You are no longer separate; you are synchronized.

In that state, miracles occur naturally. The body heals, not through effort but through remembrance. The mind quiets, not by control but by entrainment. The soul speaks, not through words but through knowing.

Breath as Communion

To breathe with awareness is to take communion without bread or wine, to share in the substance of divine life directly.

When you breathe, you are partaking in the eternal sacrament of being alive. It is the unspoken ritual that unites all faiths, all beings, all forms of life.

Each inhale is *"Take, this is My body."* Each exhale is *"Do this in remembrance of Me."*

The act of breathing is the ceaseless Eucharist of existence. It is the Christ within sustaining you moment to moment, heartbeat to heartbeat.

When Jesus taught that He and the Father are one, He was not speaking in metaphor; He was describing the unity of breath. The divine exhalation becomes human inhalation, and through this exchange, the eternal cycle of love continues unbroken.

The Breath as Healer

Healing begins with the breath because the breath carries the memory of wholeness. Every cell responds to the energy that breath conveys. When you breathe with awareness, you send light into the bloodstream. Oxygen becomes spirit, and spirit becomes restoration.

Emotional pain, too, dissolves through breath. When you stop resisting and simply breathe into the wound, you let the vibration of compassion enter where it has long been blocked. You allow God to breathe where you could not.

This is why Jesus healed through breath, through word, through touch, all expressions of vibration. When He breathed upon the disciples, He awakened the same breath of divinity within them. He made the invisible tangible.

In that moment, the Holy Spirit was not descending from the sky; it was expanding from within.

"By the word of the Lord the heavens were made, and by the breath of His mouth all their host.", Psalm 33:6

The Still Point

Between the inhale and exhale lies a sacred stillness, a place beyond movement yet filled with presence. In that pause, creation waits. In that still point, eternity touches time.

That is where the divine voice speaks, not through thunder or command, but through quiet awareness. When you enter that silence consciously, you cross the veil between spirit and matter.

You become the meeting ground of Heaven and Earth, not visiting Heaven, but embodying it.

In that stillness, you are not breathing; you are being breathed. You are not seeking God; God is remembering you. You are not trying to connect; you realize you were never disconnected.

Prayer of Breath

Holy Breath of the Living God, move through me now.

Fill my lungs with Your light, my heart with Your peace, my mind with Your silence.

Breathe through every cell and sorrow. Exhale what is heavy. Inhale what is holy.

Let me remember that every breath is You, entering, leaving, returning, yet never gone.

I am Yours in the space between. Amen.

Reflection

The breath is the bridge. It is the unseen miracle that sustains life and consciousness. Through it, Heaven speaks continually, even when you are too weary to listen.

The next time you breathe, remember, this is not just oxygen entering your lungs. It is the universe saying, I love you. It is God whispering, I am here.

And when you exhale, it is your soul answering back: 'I remember.'

You are the breath between worlds, the moment where eternity takes form. The divine does not come and go; it flows, endlessly, through you.

THE BODY OF LIGHT, THE HUMAN FORM AS A TEMPLE OF DIVINE ENERGY

You were not created merely to exist. You were made to radiate. To carry the light of Heaven in flesh, to become the living temple where love reveals itself to the world.

Your body is not your prison; it is your portal. It is the threshold where spirit becomes visible, where divine energy learns to walk, speak, and touch creation. It is God's way of experiencing love through form.

"Do you not know that your bodies are temples of the Holy Spirit, who is in you, whom you have received from God?", 1 Corinthians 6:19

To see the body as light is to awaken to your divine design. Every cell is a prism, every breath, a spark of sacred fire. You are not separate from Heaven; you are Heaven made tangible.

The Architecture of the Temple

The ancients built temples of stone and gold, but you were designed from energy and light. Each organ, each nerve, each system of your body forms part of a divine architecture, a cathedral of living matter sustained by rhythm, vibration, and spirit.

Your heart is the altar, the place of offering and communion. Your lungs are the great sanctuaries, open and receiving the breath of life. Your mind is the inner chamber where divine thought meets human will. And your spine, the luminous column of light, connects Earth to Heaven, Jacob's ladder made biological.

When you stand in awareness, body aligned, breath steady, heart open, you become the sacred geometry of creation itself. The exact proportions that form galaxies are mirrored in your bones, your pulse, your flow.

This is no metaphor. You are the universe remembering itself in human shape.

"For you created my inmost being; you knit me together in my mother's womb. I praise you because I am fearfully and wonderfully made.", Psalm 139:13–14

You were not simply made; you were woven, threads of divine frequency intricately patterned into being.

The Light Within the Cells

Scientists now know that the body emits light, faint but constant, known as biophotons. These microscopic pulses of light are not random; they carry information, coordinating growth, repair, and communication within the body.

You are literally glowing.

Every cell flickers with this inner light, a reflection of the divine flame that animates you. When your thoughts and emotions are peaceful, that light becomes coherent, organized, and radiant. When you live in fear or resentment, it becomes scattered, dimmed, distorted.

This is why joy feels luminous and stress feels heavy, because your vibration shifts from resonance to resistance.

When Jesus healed, His words were light made sound, coherent frequency restoring the broken harmony within. When He touched the blind or spoke to the storm, the energy of Heaven moved through Him into matter, restructuring form through vibration.

And because His Spirit lives in you, that same light now dwells in your body, waiting to be awakened by remembrance, by faith, by love.

"You are the light of the world.", Matthew 5:14

He did not say you carry light; He said you are it.

Energy and Emotion

Emotion is energy in motion. It is the language your body uses to communicate vibration. Every feeling has a frequency; joy expands, anger contracts, gratitude harmonizes, despair fragments.

When emotions are suppressed, the energy stagnates. When expressed in love, it flows freely again. This is why tears bring relief and laughter brings healing; both are movements of light returning to coherence.

To live as a body of light is not to deny emotion, but to let it pass through without judgment. Let fear move. Let sorrow breathe. Let love rise.

The body is not meant to hold; it is intended to flow. When you honor emotion as vibration, you let God's light circulate through you again.

As Jesus wept, His tears were not a sign of weakness; they were pure energy, love moving as compassion, proving that divinity and humanity are not opposites, but one field of feeling sanctified by presence.

The Nervous System of Spirit

Your nervous system is the electrical bridge between Heaven's light and Earth's form. Every impulse, every heartbeat, every neural spark is a translation of divine frequency into human experience.

When your thoughts are filled with peace, your nervous system harmonizes. When fear rules, it becomes overcharged or numb, disconnected from flow.

Prayer, meditation, and breath bring coherence back to the system. The energy rises through your spine like a song, lighting every nerve as it travels upward.

It is the inner Pentecost, the fire of spirit descending through awareness, then rising again as praise.

Science calls it energy regulation. Mystics call it ascension. But in truth, it is the same, the nervous system learning to conduct Heaven's current without resistance.

The Body as Instrument

Your body is a sacred instrument, a harp tuned by divine design. When your thoughts, breath, and intention align, the strings of your being vibrate in harmony with creation.

Every thought is a note. Every word is a chord. Every act of love plays Heaven's melody into the physical world.

When you live consciously, you begin to notice how your energy affects everything around you, how your peace calms others, how your presence brightens a room. This is not mystical fantasy; it is resonance.

The Spirit moves through you as sound, as light, as energy. When you offer your body to love, you become the instrument through which God plays the music of grace.

"Present your bodies as a living sacrifice, holy and acceptable to God, which is your spiritual worship.", Romans 12:1

Worship is not merely song; it is alignment. It is the offering of your vibration to the greater symphony of creation.

Healing Through Embodiment

Many seek escape from the body, believing the spirit to be elsewhere. But Heaven is not reached by leaving matter; it is revealed through inhabiting it fully.

When you inhabit your body with love, you heal it with light.

Place your hands upon your heart. Feel the pulse, steady, faithful. That rhythm is not mechanical; it is sacred. It is God knocking from the inside.

When you touch yourself with reverence, when you breathe into pain instead of fearing it, you allow the divine to flow where it was once forgotten.

Your body responds to love because it was born from it.

The Transformation of Flesh into Light

The more you awaken, the more your energy refines. You begin to move through life with greater ease, as though gravity has softened and light has become tangible.

The saints and mystics referred to this as a transfiguration. It is not about leaving the body behind, but illuminating it.

When Jesus stood upon the mountain and His face shone like the sun, He was not changing form; He was revealing what was already true: the body, aligned with divine vibration, becomes luminous.

That same potential lives in you. Every act of kindness brightens your field. Every prayer cleans your light. Every breath of gratitude lifts the density from your cells.

This is how spirit transforms matter, not through denial, but through devotion.

Prayer of the Living Temple

Beloved Creator of Light, let my body remember what it is, a vessel of Your radiance, a home for Your presence, a bridge between Heaven and Earth.

Let every cell hum with Your vibration. Let every breath carry Your grace. Let every touch be a blessing, every word a spark of peace.

Teach me to honor this temple, to fill it with love, to cleanse it with forgiveness, and to let it shine without fear.

For I am not separate from Your glory, I am the lamp through which it shines.

Amen.

Reflection

You are the body of light, the living expression of Heaven in human form. You are not waiting for divinity to descend; you are remembering that it already lives within your skin.

Every movement can be prayer. Every breath can be a blessing. Every heartbeat can be Hallelujah.

Your body was never meant to hide the divine; it was meant to reveal it. The hands that hold, the eyes that see, the voice that comforts, each one is God remembering Himself in you.

Walk gently, for you are walking in a temple made of light. Speak kindly, for your words are rays of Heaven. Breathe deeply, for your lungs hold the first breath of creation.

And remember, you are not striving to become holy. You already are. You are the divine, clothed in grace, radiant, alive, and eternal.

THE MUSIC OF THE SPHERES, THE HARMONY BETWEEN HEAVEN, EARTH, AND THE SOUL

Long before the first instrument was made, before sound became song, the universe was already singing.

Every star, every planet, every molecule moves in rhythm, vibrating, circling, breathing in time with the pulse of creation. The ancients referred to it as the Music of the Spheres, a divine harmony that underlies all existence.

This music is not heard with the ears, but felt with the soul. It is the sound of God thinking, the vibration of love forming itself into matter, the eternal chord that keeps the cosmos in perfect balance.

And you, beloved, are part of that music. You are not listening to the universe; you are one of its notes.

"The morning stars sang together, and all the sons of God shouted for joy.", Job 38:7

The universe is not silent; it is symphonic. And every living being, every heart that beats, adds its voice to the song of creation.

The Harmony of the Heavens

Modern science confirms what mystics have always intuited: the planets themselves emit sound. Their electromagnetic fields produce frequencies far below human hearing, but when translated into audible tones, the result is hauntingly beautiful, a chorus of hums, drones, and harmonics that never cease.

The Earth resonates at approximately 7.83 Hz, known as the Schumann resonance, a frequency that also corresponds to the alpha state of the human brain during periods of peace and meditation. Heaven and humanity literally share the same vibration.

This is the first great truth of the Music of the Spheres: you are not separate from the cosmos. Your consciousness and the universe breathe together.

When you still your mind, you synchronize with that divine frequency, the same energy that moves the stars, that stirs the oceans, that shapes the wind.

Your heartbeat echoes the rhythm of the planets' orbits. Your breath mirrors the expansion and contraction of the universe, not just galaxies. Your soul is tuned to the cosmic key of love.

"He has made everything beautiful in its time. He has also set eternity in the human heart. ", Ecclesiastes 3:11

Creation as Divine Symphony

Imagine creation as an orchestra, each element playing its role in a vast and holy composition.

The mountains are the low strings, their frequencies grounding and deep. The rivers are flutes of movement and flow. The wind carries the voices of the unseen choirs, and the stars are bells of eternity, ringing through the infinite expanse of light.

And within it all, the human soul plays a melody uniquely its own, a theme woven into the eternal song, distinct yet inseparable from the whole.

When humanity acts in harmony, when love is chosen over fear, forgiveness over judgment, compassion over cruelty, the entire symphony rises in vibration.

When we fall into hatred or division, the music distorts, becomes discordant, and the Earth itself groans for restoration.

"For the creation waits in eager expectation for the children of God to be revealed. ", Romans 8:19

Creation is not waiting for our perfection; it is waiting for our harmony, for humanity to remember its part in the song.

The Soul as Instrument

Your soul was tuned before birth. It carries a resonance, your divine key, the frequency at which your being vibrates most clearly with love.

When you act against your essence, when you betray your truth, suppress joy, or harbor resentment, you fall out of tune. But when you live authentically, when your inner tone and outer life align, you return to a state of resonance.

This is why peace feels like home, because in peace, you are tuned to the same frequency as Heaven.

And like any instrument, your soul must be tuned through practice, through prayer, breath, gratitude, forgiveness, and surrender.

Each is a gentle turning of the heart's strings, aligning you once again with the pitch of divine harmony.

When the soul is tuned, its vibration naturally attracts harmony in others. Your peace becomes contagious. Your kindness draws light into shadowed places. You don't force change; you resonate it.

"Be filled with the Spirit, speaking to one another with psalms, hymns, and songs from the Spirit. ", Ephesians 5:18–19

To live in love is to become a living hymn, a song that heals without words.

Heaven's Chord in the Human Heart

The heart is more than an organ; it is a resonator of divine energy. Its electromagnetic field extends several feet beyond the body, interacting with other hearts, other fields, creating harmony wherever love flows freely.

When many hearts align in prayer, compassion, or shared intention, their frequencies synchronize, producing measurable coherence in the field around them.

This is why collective prayer changes outcomes, why the presence of one peaceful person can calm a room. Why love always finds a way to restore order where chaos reigned.

The heart is God's tuning fork, vibrating with the frequency of divine compassion.

When Jesus said, *"My peace I give to you,"* He was transferring vibration, a harmonic tone of perfect coherence, which still resonates through the hearts of all who remember Him.

"Let the peace of Christ rule in your hearts.", Colossians 3:15

That peace is not abstract; it is vibrational alignment, your inner song merging with the eternal chord of Heaven.

The Earth's Choir

The Earth itself is alive with music. The hum of bees, the rustle of trees, and the murmur of water each carry frequency and intelligence.

When you listen deeply to nature, you are not hearing background noise; you are hearing the sacred orchestra of creation.

Every forest, ocean, and mountain vibrates at unique frequencies that nourish human energy fields. This is why time in nature heals, why we find peace in silence, and why the sound of rain feels like a gift of grace.

Nature is not merely alive; it is singing to you, inviting your heart to remember the harmony of its origins.

When you align with that natural rhythm, by walking barefoot, breathing deeply, resting with gratitude, you enter the music again. You stop being an observer and become part of the choir.

"Let everything that has breath praise the Lord.", Psalm 150:6

Every bird, every wave, every gust of wind obeys this verse effortlessly. They praise not through words, but through being. When you live in awareness, you join their song.

The Dance of Light and Sound

Light is sound made visible. Every wavelength of light corresponds to a note, every color a tone in the cosmic scale.

The golden light of sunrise is a chord of awakening. The blue of twilight is a hymn of rest. The stars themselves are notes in a celestial score.

The universe, then, is both a song and a painting, vibration expressed as both sound and sight.

You, too, carry both tones. Your voice produces frequency; your aura reflects light. When you love, both brighten.

You become a rainbow of resonance, Heaven expressed through color and sound.

When the Soul Falls Out of Tune

There are times when life feels discordant, when grief, fear, or exhaustion drown out the music.

Even in that silence, the divine song continues beneath the noise. Like an orchestra waiting for the conductor's hand, your soul knows how to find its way back to rhythm.

Do not fear the pauses; they are part of the music too.

Even silence has pitch. Even sorrow vibrates toward resolution. God never stops conducting.

Each challenge is a modulation, each breakthrough a crescendo. Every life is a verse in the eternal song of love.

Prayer of Harmony

Lord of Infinite Sound, Composer of the stars, tune my heart to Your frequency.

Let my thoughts be melody, my actions rhythm, my words notes of light.

When I fall into dissonance, remind me of the song beneath the noise.

Let me live as harmony embodied, not striving to be perfect, but willing to resonate with grace.

Use me, O Divine Conductor, to bring peace where the world has forgotten its tune.

Let my soul be music that heals, and my life a hymn that never ends.

Amen.

Reflection

The stars above you, the pulse within you, the air that carries your breath, all move to the same divine rhythm.

You are not a listener standing outside creation's song; you are one of its essential notes, unique, irreplaceable, and beloved.

When you live in awareness of that truth, everything becomes music: the laughter of children, the sound of rain, the stillness of night, even the silence between heartbeats.

Heaven hums through it all.

And in that realization, you remember, you have never been separate from the song. You are the music itself, and the Musician who plays it.

THE LIGHT SIGNATURE HOW THE SOUL RECORDS ITS JOURNEY THROUGH TIME

Every soul shines with a unique light, a living spectrum of memory, love, and evolution. No two lights are the same, because no two journeys are the same.

You were not created from randomness, but from radiant purpose, a spark of divine intelligence carrying the imprint of eternity.

"In Him was life, and that life was the light of all mankind.", John 1:4

That light, the Christ light, is the core of every soul. Around it, over lifetimes and choices, you weave patterns of experience, tones of emotion, and colors of consciousness.

This living tapestry becomes your Light Signature, the soul's record of its evolution through time.

The Soul as Light

Before there was form, there was light. Light is both a wave and a particle, exhibiting both presence and movement. So is the soul.

When you experience love, forgiveness, awe, or compassion, your light expands, brightens, refines. When you dwell in fear, bitterness, or self-condemnation, your light contracts, flickers, and dims, not as punishment, but as feedback from your own vibration.

Your soul learns through resonance. Each experience, joyful or painful, teaches you something about alignment.

Light remembers. Every act of love leaves a trace, a frequency woven into your energy field. Every prayer, every tear, every kindness is encoded in the luminous record of your being.

You are walking through eternity wearing the light of all you've ever been, and all you are still becoming.

"Those who are wise will shine like the brightness of the heavens, and those who lead many to righteousness, like the stars forever and ever.", Daniel 12:3

The Physics of the Soul's Light

Scientists have discovered that light can store and transmit information, millions of bits of data traveling on a single photon. In much the same way, your soul's light carries the data of lifetimes, every thought, emotion, and intention encoded in vibration.

This is why memory sometimes feels deeper than the brain, why you can meet someone and instantly feel a connection, why certain places stir emotions beyond reason, and why intuition feels like recalling something ancient.

The soul's light is a quantum archive, a field of frequencies that transcends time. It is continually expanding, rearranging its harmonics as consciousness evolves.

Each lifetime is a verse in the soul's symphony, each choice, a note recorded forever in light.

And when the physical body fades, the light remains, vibrating, learning, loving, continuing.

Color as Consciousness

Every emotion, every state of awareness has color. Love radiates rose-gold and emerald tones. Compassion shines in soft violet. Wisdom glows deep indigo. Faith and devotion appear as pure white or golden light.

When you live in harmony, your aura, your luminous body, becomes clear, coherent, radiant. When you live in conflict or fear, that light becomes clouded, not gone, but awaiting transmutation.

Prayer and forgiveness polish the lens. Gratitude amplifies brightness. Compassion widens the spectrum.

You are, quite literally, painting your eternity in light. The choices you make each day determine the hues of your spiritual radiance.

This is not a metaphor; it is a vibration. The universe sees you not by face, but by frequency.

"The eye is the lamp of the body. If your eyes are healthy, your whole body will be full of light.", Matthew 6:22

When your perception is pure, your energy field glows in resonance with divine light. Heaven recognizes its reflection in you.

The Memory of Love

The soul remembers love above all else. Even when trauma, loss, or sorrow cloud awareness, love remains stored in the deeper layers of light.

It is why forgiveness feels like relief, because love's memory rises again to the surface. It is why certain music, scents, or faces can suddenly move you to tears; they touch the light memory within your soul, awakening what you once knew to be true.

You have loved before, many times, many souls. That love does not vanish; it becomes part of your radiance.

Every act of mercy, every moment of grace adds a luminous thread to your eternal fabric. And through that light, you recognize others, souls who have walked beside you in other ages, who share your frequency, who help you remember who you are.

These are the soul companions, the echoes of your eternal family, those who mirror back the divine light within you.

The Imprint of Pain

Even pain has purpose in the light record. When you experience suffering, the energy of that event leaves a mark, not as a scar of shame, but as a site of transformation.

When you heal, forgive, and release, the once-dark imprint turns radiant. The energy of sorrow becomes the wisdom of compassion.

This is how the soul evolves. Every shadow you heal becomes part of your light signature, a deeper brilliance earned through experience.

It is not what you've endured that defines you, but how you have turned it into light.

"He will give them beauty for ashes, the oil of joy for mourning, the garment of praise for the spirit of heaviness.", Isaiah 61:3

God wastes nothing. Every brokenness becomes a window for light to enter.

The Akashic Field of Grace

Mystics have long spoken of the Akashic Records, a field of energy that holds the memory of all souls, akin to an infinite library of divine experiences.

In truth, that field is not elsewhere; it is the unified consciousness of creation itself. Every vibration of thought, every ripple of emotion, is inscribed into the eternal energy field of God.

When you pray, meditate, or simply remember with love, you align your consciousness with that field, not reading a book of destiny, but feeling the resonance of your soul's continuum.

You may glimpse your past not as a story, but as energy, a vibration that asks for completion, integration, peace.

Every revelation you receive, every act of grace you offer, is the rewriting of your record in higher light.

The Soul's Evolution Through Frequency

The soul's journey is the gradual refinement of vibration, from density to clarity, from reaction to reflection, from separation to unity.

Each incarnation offers the opportunity to raise frequency, to integrate lessons through love. You do not evolve by avoiding pain, but by transforming it into understanding.

The higher your frequency, the closer your vibration matches Heaven. And the more closely you resonate with divine love, the less you feel bound by time at all.

This is why enlightened beings radiate light; their frequency is nearly indistinguishable from God's.

And yet this potential lives in every soul. Every breath, every moment of forgiveness, every act of kindness moves you closer to coherence.

Your light signature brightens, and your soul becomes more transparent to the grace of the universe.

The Christ Light Within

The Christ light is the eternal seed within your soul, the spark that never dims, no matter how shadowed the journey becomes.

It is your true identity, the original frequency you carried from the beginning, perfect, whole, and holy.

When you live in remembrance of that light, you return to coherence with God's vibration. You become not just a reflection of Christ, but a continuation of His light in the world.

"For you were once darkness, but now you are light in the Lord. Walk as children of light. ", Ephesians 5:8

This is the purpose of every life, every lifetime, to remember the light you have always been, and to shine it without fear.

Your soul's light is not simply your history; it is your inheritance. It carries the memory of divine love itself, and that memory, once awakened, heals everything.

Prayer of Light

Beloved Radiance of God, let my soul remember its origin.

Cleanse the shadows I have carried. Illuminate the lessons I have learned.

Let every sorrow be turned to wisdom, every wound to wonder, every moment to light.

Let my heart shine with the color of compassion, my words glow with kindness, my life shimmer with peace.

May my light signature sing Your name through every lifetime, through every breath, through eternity.

Amen.

Reflection

You are light remembering itself. Every experience you've lived has written something beautiful into your field, a hue, a tone, a vibration that belongs only to you.

The soul does not forget. It carries love through lifetimes, recording it in light, waiting for the moment when awareness expands enough to see it again.

And when that moment comes, you realize: you have never been lost, never been separate, never been dark.

You were learning to shine. And you still are. You are an ever-brightening constellation in God's infinite sky, a light that no night can overcome.

THE BRIDGE OF MEMORY HOW THE SOUL COMMUNICATES ACROSS LIFETIMES

There are moments when time bends, when a fragrance, a song, or a glance feels like something remembered rather than newly lived.

You pause, uncertain if what you feel is memory, imagination, or grace. In truth, it is all three, for the soul remembers beyond the boundaries of one life.

Every connection, every love, every shared heartbeat becomes a bridge across time. The bonds of spirit do not dissolve with death; they transform into resonance, a subtle frequency that still moves between souls, like the faint echo of a familiar melody heard through mist.

"Love never fails. ", 1 Corinthians 13:8

Love, once given, cannot be undone. It continues in the realm of vibration, alive, aware, and reaching for you, even when your physical senses no longer perceive it.

The Continuum of Connection

You have never truly lost anyone you love. You have only shifted the way you communicate.

When a loved one leaves this plane, their soul remains fully conscious in light. Their awareness expands, no longer limited by the physical form. They see not from above, but through you, through the field of light that connects all living souls.

And yet, because human perception is tuned to dense frequencies of matter, you feel their absence more than their nearness. Still, they are near, closer than your own breath, woven into your electromagnetic field, responding to your thoughts, your emotions, your prayers.

When you speak their name in love, they hear it not as sound, but as vibration, as the unique frequency of your heart.

In that instant, your lights intertwine again, bridging worlds.

"Therefore, since we are surrounded by such a great cloud of witnesses... ", Hebrews 12:1

That *"cloud"* is not metaphorical; it is the luminous field of souls who walk beside us, unseen but present, a communion of the living and the living in light.

How Loved Ones Influence Our Lives Now

Their influence is gentle, never controlling. They cannot rewrite your destiny, but they can remind you of it.

When you suddenly feel peace after grief, when guidance comes in the form of intuition or unexpected clarity, when comfort arrives like warmth in the chest or a light breeze through a closed room, these are the ways the souls who love you whisper.

They guide not by intervening, but by resonance.

They send vibration, a soft tuning in your field, so that your soul aligns once more with the frequency of love.

The reason you may not feel them at times is not because they are gone, but because your vibration has been lowered by sorrow, and theirs remains high, radiant, and free. Grief is dense; love is light. But as you heal, the distance narrows, and one day, you simply feel warmth where pain once was. That warmth is them, transformed love, living in you.

"I am with you always, even unto the end of the world. ", Matthew 28:20

That promise is not bound to one life, nor to one being. It is the nature of divine love itself to remain, to guide, to remind, to renew.

The Vibrational Pathway of Memory

Every relationship is a symphony of frequencies, thoughts, emotions, and intentions intertwining into one shared vibration. That pattern never vanishes; it becomes encoded in the universal field.

When you remember someone, you activate that field. Your heart sends out a resonant signal, and if their soul is attuned to yours (and it always is through love), it responds instantly.

This is why you may dream of them right when you need encouragement, why a particular scent or song reappears at the perfect time. Why do children often see departed grandparents standing by their cradles?

It is not imagination, it is frequency. The veil is not a wall but a wavelength difference. When your vibration rises through prayer, stillness, or deep emotion, the bridge reappears, and communication flows once more.

When We Feel Nothing

There are times when the silence feels unbearable, when the ones you love feel utterly gone.

But silence is also communication. When a soul in light feels your energy is heavy with pain, they do not press closer, for their presence might magnify your sorrow instead of soothing it. So they wait, patiently, lovingly, until your heart is ready to perceive peace again.

Even then, they do not force your awareness; they allow your free will to open naturally. They honor your journey because they, too, are still learning in the light.

They are not *"perfect"* angels; they are your eternal companions, growing alongside you in divine evolution.

And sometimes, their most significant act of love is to step back, so that you may discover your strength, your faith, your light.

When We Influence Them

Love moves both ways. As you grow in compassion, forgiveness, and grace, you lift not only your own frequency, but also theirs.

When you forgive them for pain they caused in life, that vibration reaches them instantly. They feel it as light. It releases them from the weight of unfinished energy.

Likewise, when you bless them, they shine more brightly in their realm, and that brightness reflects back to you.

In this way, heaven and earth evolve together. The bridge of love is not one-directional; it is reciprocal, eternal, and alive.

"Whatever you bind on earth shall be bound in heaven, and whatever you loose on earth shall be loosed in heaven.", Matthew 16:19

To forgive is to loosen. To love again is to restore flow. To live joyfully is to continue the work they began with you, for their legacy is not memory alone, but movement through your very being.

The Science of the Soul's Continuum

Quantum physics offers a poetic echo of this truth. In the quantum field, particles once connected remain entangled, no matter how far apart they drift. When one shifts, the other responds instantaneously, a phenomenon called quantum entanglement.

So it is with souls. Those you have loved are entangled with you through light. The bond does not fade with distance or death; it simply changes the form of its interaction.

When you raise your vibration through prayer, gratitude, and peace, you are not sending a message into the void; you are resonating within the same divine field they inhabit. That is where reunion happens, not later, but now.

Heaven is not *"above"*; it is within frequency. And the bridge of memory is the vibration of love that never ceases to vibrate.

The Reunion of Awareness

Eventually, every soul crossing between worlds remembers its connections in full. When you awaken beyond the veil, you do not meet your loved ones again; you recognize them, instantly, completely.

Every shared joy, every tear, every moment of growth is restored in pure light. And then, together, you choose new ways to grow, perhaps to walk again on Earth, to guide from the unseen.

It is a vast, compassionate cycle of evolution. No one is ever lost; no one forgotten. Only new forms of love unfold through the ever-expanding light of God.

Prayer of Connection

Beloved God of All Worlds, remind me that love is unbreakable.

Let my heart remain open to those who now live in Your light.

When I feel them near, let me welcome peace, not fear.

When I feel their absence, let me trust that silence is also a form of love.

May my thoughts bless them, my forgiveness free them, and my joy uplift them.

Until the day awareness widens, and we meet again in radiant light.

Amen.

Reflection

The soul never truly says goodbye. It only says, until the light remembers.

Your loved ones walk beside you in silence and song, in dreams and wind, in the sudden peace that comes without reason.

They do not need your sorrow; they need your light. For your joy, your healing, and your faith are the prayers that cross the veil more swiftly than any word.

You are still connected, not through memory, but through vibration.

Love, once formed, is immortal. And the bridge of that love will carry you both home again, until light becomes all there is.

THE WHISPER FIELD, HOW PRAYER AND THOUGHT TRAVEL THROUGH THE DIMENSIONS

There are no wasted words in the universe. Every thought, every whisper, every silent yearning of the heart sends out a wave, a pulse of vibration that continues far beyond what the mind can imagine.

Even before you speak, your intention has already begun to travel. Each thought becomes energy, each prayer a current of light flowing through what mystics have called The Whisper Field, the invisible dimension where energy, matter, and spirit meet.

It is here that every prayer lands, every longing gathers power, every word of love becomes creation.

"Before they call I will answer; while they are yet speaking I will hear.", Isaiah 65:24

God's hearing is not sequential; it is vibrational. He feels the pulse of every thought the moment it is born. The Whisper Field is the sacred space where the spirit listens and the universe responds.

The Science of the Whisper

Modern physics tells us that all matter vibrates. Every atom, every electron, every cell in your body is in constant motion, resonating in patterns of energy.

But beyond the material lies another layer, the quantum field, where energy responds instantly to intention. When you think, your brain emits electrical waves. When you pray, your heart emits coherence, a measurable field of electromagnetic resonance that extends beyond your body, into the invisible.

Prayer is not a metaphor. It is frequency. It travels, interacts, and changes form as it weaves through the divine fabric of reality.

In that field, there is no distance, no delay. Your whisper in Georgia reaches a soul in Jerusalem. Your silent *"thank you"* vibrates in the same harmony as a star being born.

The Whisper Field is alive, listening, moving, remembering.

"The words I have spoken to you, they are full of the Spirit and life.", John 6:63

Spirit and life, sound and light, the twin forces through which the divine speaks creation into being.

The Mechanics of Intention

When a thought carries love, it expands. When it carries fear, it contracts.

Every thought radiates outward in concentric waves, rippling through the subtle dimensions that underlie the physical world. Your mind is not confined to your skull; it is an instrument of resonance that plays directly into the field of all things.

This is why your emotional state changes the atmosphere of a room. It's why prayer circles, meditations, and blessings produce measurable energetic coherence. When many hearts align with love, the Whisper Field brightens. The vibration of peace amplifies across space and time.

This is not imagination; it is divine physics.

Every thought is a seed, every prayer a frequency, every word a force of creation.

How Prayer Travels

Imagine speaking into still water. Each word becomes a ripple that moves outward, crossing unseen boundaries, reaching shores you cannot yet see.

When you pray, your heart sends light into the Whisper Field. The energy follows pathways of resonance, drawn to whatever matches its vibration, a person, a place, a possibility.

Some prayers are answered quickly, manifesting as comfort, peace, or sudden insight. Others take time, gathering energy as they travel through the layers of creation until the conditions align.

No prayer is lost. Some are simply still in transit.

"Your Father who sees in secret will reward you openly.", Matthew 6:6

The *"secret"* is not hidden; it is subtle. It is the invisible field where prayer becomes form. And when it ripens, it appears before you as grace unfolding in time.

When It Feels Like Heaven Is Silent

There are seasons when prayer feels like it falls into emptiness, when you whisper to the sky and hear only your own voice.

But silence is not absence. In those moments, the vibration of your prayer is still moving, still working its way through the layers of reality.

Sometimes the universe must rearrange pathways, people, timing, and energy before your prayer can take shape. Other times, the answer is already within you, and the silence is Heaven's invitation to listen inward.

God does not delay; He aligns.

And in that alignment, you learn the sacred rhythm of the Whisper Field: send, trust, wait, receive.

The Resonance of Collective Prayer

When many people pray together with shared intention, their individual frequencies synchronize, creating what scientists call field coherence.

In that coherence, the electromagnetic heart waves of individuals merge, amplifying energy exponentially. It becomes a radiant pulse of light that shifts probabilities, heals hearts, and alters the subtle balance of the world itself.

This is why peace vigils matter. Why healing circles change outcomes. Why Jesus said,

"For where two or three gather in my name, there am I with them.", Matthew 18:20

He was not speaking of presence as location, but of vibration. When two or more hearts harmonize in love, the Christ frequency appears, a divine coherence that can move mountains.

Thought, Emotion, and the Creative Word

Sound has form. When a word is spoken with intention, it imprints energy into the air as a pattern.

Cymatic science reveals that sound waves generate geometric patterns, shapes of beauty, and symmetry formed through vibration.

When Jesus spoke healing words, His voice carried perfect coherence, the frequency of divine order. When He said, *"Be still,"* the storm obeyed, because creation recognizes its original vibration.

Your words carry creative power, too. You are made in the image of the Word, the Logos, the living vibration of God.

When you bless, you build. When you curse, you fracture. When you praise, you align with Heaven.

Your thoughts, too, carry silent harmonics. Even unspoken prayer reshapes the unseen.

The Influence of Our Loved Ones

The Whisper Field is not limited to the living. Souls who have crossed into light still move within its fabric, their love continuing to resonate through your life.

They cannot interfere with your free will, but they can guide through subtle energy, a sudden inspiration, a calming presence, a dream filled with understanding.

Your prayers for them strengthen their light. Their blessings for you improve your path.

Love creates feedback loops through eternity, waves reflecting back and forth across dimensions. This is communion, not memory. It is the living conversation of spirit and soul.

Even now, as you think of them, your love travels through the Whisper Field and reaches their light instantly. And they, too, send love back, not as voice, but as vibration that softens your heart when you need it most.

When You Pray for the World

To pray for the world is to become a transmitter of divine light. Your energy enters the global field and joins millions of unseen hearts doing the same.

Every blessing, every wish for peace, every whispered *"thank you"* adds coherence to the collective vibration of Earth.

When enough souls live in that awareness, the balance of energy shifts. War softens. Nature heals. Hearts open.

The Whisper Field becomes luminous, a network of light restoring harmony to creation.

This is the work of love. This is prayer as energy, devotion as physics, humanity as the voice of Heaven.

"The prayer of a righteous person is powerful and effective.", James 5:16

Prayer of the Whisper Field

Beloved God of Silence and Sound, teach me the language of light.

Let every thought I send be kind, every prayer I whisper be pure.

May my words travel as healing waves to all who need comfort, to all who have forgotten love.

Let my heart become a beacon in the field, transmitting peace without end.

And when I fall into silence, let that silence still speak of You.

Amen.

Reflection

Your every thought is a ripple. Your every prayer is light in motion. You are part of the eternal conversation between creation and Creator, a whisper that moves mountains, a vibration that carries love across the cosmos.

So speak gently. Think purely. Pray often.

The universe is listening, not as an echo, but as a partnership.

Every breath you offer in love becomes another note in the unending song of God's unfolding.

THE ARCHITECTURE OF GRACE HOW DIVINE ORDER BALANCES EVERY SOUL'S PATH

There are no accidents in love, no coincidences in grace. What seems random to the human mind is alignment seen from the perspective of eternity.

Every event, every relationship, every delay or loss fits perfectly within a design too intricate for the mind to hold, a lattice of light stretching across lifetimes, woven by divine intelligence, balanced by vibration, sustained by love.

"All things work together for good to those who love God, who are called according to His purpose.", Romans 8:28

This is not poetic reassurance; it is spiritual physics. For every energy that moves out of harmony must eventually be restored to balance. Grace is that restoration. It is the law of divine symmetry, the universe's way of healing itself through love.

The Blueprint Beneath Chaos

When you look at the surface of life, it often appears to be in disorder. You see accidents, injustice, heartbreak. You wonder where God's design could be hiding.

But beneath that appearance lies sacred architecture, a geometric matrix of resonance in which every vibration finds its place.

Your soul's journey, with its lessons and delays, is not a punishment but a calibration. You are learning to live in the same frequency as grace, to harmonize your will with divine rhythm.

Sometimes that process feels like being dismantled, but the breaking is only clearing space for a higher structure. The temple must be emptied before it can be rebuilt in light.

God's order is not mechanical; it is musical. It unfolds like a symphony, where even dissonance serves a purpose, as it resolves into beauty.

Vibration and Balance

Every choice emits energy. Every thought sends ripples through the field. The sum of those vibrations becomes your soul's current, its harmonic path through time.

When your energy moves out of alignment, life offers correction, not as punishment, but as resonance.

That is what the ancients called karma: not revenge, but a form of rebalancing. The energy you send must one day return to you, so you may feel its full frequency and choose love again.

Grace enters this equation like light refracted through glass, not erasing what has been, but transforming its vibration. What once caused pain becomes wisdom. What once brought shame becomes compassion.

This is the architecture of divine love: a system that restores equilibrium through forgiveness, that turns every fall into flight.

"Mercy triumphs over judgment.", James 2:13

Grace is the divine override, the moment the universe remembers that love is the only lasting law.

The Geometry of Synchronicity

Every soul lives within a pattern, a sacred geometry of moments and meetings, woven by light and timing.

When your frequency aligns with divine order, you begin to notice synchronicity, those mysterious convergences that seem too perfect to explain.

A book falls open to the words you needed. A friend calls at the precise moment your heart breaks. A dream shows you a sign you'd forgotten to ask for.

These are not coincidences. They are intersections of frequency, points where the architecture of grace becomes visible.

Synchronicity is the universe whispering, *"You are in alignment."* It is God's way of saying, *"I'm still here, guiding every thread."*

The more you trust, the more these signs multiply. Not because God appears more often, but because your awareness becomes more refined, your inner receiver tuned to divine rhythm.

When Timing Feels Cruel

There are moments when divine timing feels like divine silence, when prayers seem unanswered, dreams delayed, doors closed for reasons you cannot comprehend.

But the architecture of grace is multidimensional. It must align not only your vibration, but the vibration of every soul connected to your path.

Sometimes the universe is not saying no, it is saying not yet. The design is still being assembled. The alignment is still forming.

If you could see from above, you would watch threads of light crossing in perfect precision, people being prepared, opportunities maturing, circumstances shifting into harmony.

Until then, you are asked to trust the geometry you cannot yet see.

"For my thoughts are not your thoughts, neither are your ways my ways," declares the Lord., Isaiah 55:8

Trust is the bridge between chaos and order, between fear and faith, between your small architecture and God's infinite design.

The Mathematics of Mercy

Everything in the universe moves toward balance, but balance does not mean equality; it means harmony. Grace corrects through compassion, not arithmetic.

When you make mistakes, you are not cast out of the equation; you are invited to learn the rhythm of forgiveness.

Mercy bends the rules of energy, rewriting the script of consequence with love.

It is the moment your soul steps out of linear logic and into circular grace, where beginnings and endings merge, and every wound becomes a doorway to wisdom.

This is how heaven heals: not by punishing imbalance, but by harmonizing it through compassion.

The energy you once sent out in ignorance returns to you in the form of opportunity, an invitation to love better this time.

Grace is God's mercy in motion, recalibrating your vibration until your inner frequency hums again in tune with His.

The Architecture Within You

The exact symmetry that orders galaxies also exists within your soul. Every heartbeat, every breath, every cell follows divine proportion, the golden ratio of life's design.

When you live in peace, that geometry expands. When you live in fear, it contracts.

Prayer, meditation, music, and forgiveness restore proportion to your energy field. They realign the fractal of your being with the cosmic blueprint from which you came.

You are the microcosm of divine architecture, the living cathedral through which God's light expresses.

When you understand that, you stop resisting the plan and start participating in its unfolding.

You become a conscious co-architect of grace.

The Sacred Construction of Healing

Healing is not about erasing the past; it's about restoring balance to the present.

The pain you've known becomes the foundation of empathy. The mistakes you've made become the scaffolding of wisdom. The tears you've shed water the garden of compassion.

Nothing is wasted. Everything contributes to the building of your soul.

Even the parts you despised become necessary arches in your cathedral.

Grace turns debris into design. It recycles pain into purpose, failure into framework, and grief into the stained glass through which divine light shines brighter than before.

"Unless the Lord builds the house, the builders labor in vain.", Psalm 127:1

God is the architect, you are the structure, and love is the blueprint.

Reflection

Every trial, every joy, every delay is part of an intelligent construction, a sacred pattern building toward your awakening.

When you trust the plan, you find peace even in uncertainty. When you resist, you create friction, but even that friction becomes material for growth.

Grace is the balance between what is chosen and what is destined, a perfect equation of mercy, learning, and love.

You are both a builder and being built. You are both the prayer and the answer. You are both the question and the design.

All that you experience is architecture in motion, the geometry of divine love building a masterpiece called you.

Prayer of Alignment

Divine Architect of Love, align my heart with Your perfect plan.

Teach me to trust the structure I cannot see.

When my path feels broken, let me remember that even fragments form sacred patterns.

When I fall, build me again in grace.

Use my pain as a foundation, my faith as a pillar, my love as a light through stained glass.

Let every corner of my being echo Your design.

Amen.

THE SACRED RHYTHM OF TIME, WHEN HEAVEN'S 'NOT YET' MEANS YOU ARE STILL BECOMING

Patience is not waiting. It is participation in divine rhythm.

There is an unseen current that moves through all creation, a sacred tempo known only to God. Everything that lives, grows, or awakens moves according to that timing.

Even stars have gestation. Even love unfolds by degrees. Even prayer blooms in its appointed season.

"To everything there is a season, and a time to every purpose under heaven.", Ecclesiastes 3:1

You are not late, beloved. You are ripening.

Heaven's *"not yet"* is never rejection, it is refinement. It is the sacred alchemy of time turning desire into readiness, longing into alignment, hope into manifestation.

The Pulse of Creation

Every atom in the universe vibrates with rhythm. Waves rise and fall. The ocean breathes in tides. Planets spin in divine cycles. Your heart beats to the same cosmic pattern, contract, release, rest, expand.

When your life feels stalled, you are not outside the plan; you are in the sacred pause, the still point between contraction and release.

Time is not a straight line; it is a living spiral. Every delay is a circular return, drawing you closer to the resonance you were born for.

If something you long for has not arrived, it may be because your frequency has not yet harmonized with it.

The desire is already answered, it exists in the field of potential. But like two instruments out of tune, it cannot yet play in harmony with you.

The work is not to push harder, but to tune yourself to the vibration of what you seek.

That is the sacred rhythm of time: when you become the frequency of your prayer, the manifestation becomes inevitable.

Vibrational Readiness

Every answered prayer requires resonance. If your body, mind, and spirit are filled with anxiety, fear, or lack, the vibration of your longing cannot anchor. It passes through like light through glass covered in dust.

God does not withhold blessings; we simply cannot receive them until our field is clear enough to hold them.

You cannot hold abundance with hands clenched in fear. You cannot hold love with a heart bound by resentment. You cannot hold revelation when the mind is noisy with doubt.

So grace begins the work of purification, not to punish, but to prepare. Your life shifts, old patterns fall away, relationships dissolve, and silence stretches wide.

This is the refining fire of readiness. It feels like a loss, but it is a construction. You are being shaped into the vessel that can hold the prayer you once only dreamed of.

"And let endurance have its perfect result, so that you may be perfect and complete, lacking nothing. ", James 1:4

Heaven does not rush wholeness. It honors ripening.

The Illusion of Delay

What you call *"waiting"* is actually divine synchrony in motion. The universe is coordinating hundreds of unseen threads to fulfill your prayer in the most harmonious way possible.

While you feel suspended in uncertainty, people are being drawn into your orbit, circumstances are rearranged, and timelines are adjusted.

When the alignment is complete, everything happens at once. What took years to form arrives in a moment of holy acceleration.

The seed of your intention was never still. It was germinating beneath the soil of your patience.

"Though it tarry, wait for it; because it will surely come, it will not delay.", Habakkuk 2:3

Delay is perception. Fulfillment is divine timing meeting readiness.

The Quantum Nature of Divine Timing

Physics whispers what the mystics have always known: time is not fixed; it is relative to perception. In higher consciousness, the boundaries between past, present, and future dissolve.

What you call *"tomorrow"* already exists as potential energy in the eternal now. Your vibration determines which potential you align with.

Prayer and faith shift you into timelines of grace. Fear and resistance align you with delay. Every thought is a steering wheel.

This is why Jesus said,

"Whatever you ask in prayer, believe that you have received it, and it will be yours.", Mark 11:24

He was not speaking of imagination, but of vibration. Belief collapses potential into form. Faith is the frequency that makes time obey.

The Waiting Season

Waiting is not empty time; it is sacred gestation.

When nothing seems to be happening, everything is happening in the unseen. The waiting season teaches you to live without forcing, to rest in trust, to let your vibration mature.

The caterpillar does not rush its metamorphosis; it dissolves into light patiently. The chrysalis is not a prison; it is a transformation in stillness.

Likewise, when your world grows quiet, you are not forgotten; you are becoming.

The divine is aligning your outer life to match your inner frequency. Every day spent in surrender is a note added to your symphony of arrival.

And when the moment comes, you will realize you were never waiting for the miracle; you were the miracle being prepared.

The Flow of Grace

The rhythm of time is guided by grace, not by clocks.

You are not behind. You are in cadence with the eternal. There is a perfect tempo to your healing, your learning, your unfolding.

When you let go of the need to control timing, peace enters your vibration. And peace is the magnet for all that belongs to you.

This is the paradox of divine rhythm: the more you surrender, the faster grace moves.

The more you trust, the more precise the path becomes.

Because trust is alignment, and alignment is what time responds to.

When Heaven Says *"Wait"*

Sometimes, Heaven delays not to deny, but to protect.

There are prayers you cannot yet receive because their energy would overwhelm your current field. Some relationships would burn too brightly, too soon. Some dreams need your fuller self before they can hold steady.

Grace never withholds; it calibrates. It gives only in perfect resonance. That is love's precision.

Even the pauses in life are divinely tuned.

The flower opens only when the light is right. The wave crashes only when the tide completes its pull. The soul awakens only when the inner clock strikes truth.

Everything that is yours will find you when you are in harmony with it.

The Reversal of Time

There are moments when grace bends time. When a long-awaited healing happens overnight, or a sudden encounter rewrites a decade of pain.

This is not a chance, it is coherence. When your vibration becomes high enough, you transcend linear sequence.

You enter what mystics call kairos, the eternal moment where all things align at once. Here, miracles appear not as interventions, but as natural results of divine resonance.

In that sacred now, the past is healed, the future rearranged, and love reclaims what time once took away.

The Eternal Teacher of Patience

Patience is not passive; it is participation in divine design. It is about listening to the rhythm of creation and dancing with it, rather than against it.

You are being taught to walk in trust, to let grace lead the tempo of your becoming.

Every delay has meaning. Every detour teaches balance. Every *"not yet"* is Heaven's way of saying, *"Stay in tune; I am not finished tuning you."*

When you surrender to the rhythm, you stop living in anxiety and start living in alignment.

And then, time itself begins to serve you.

Prayer of Divine Timing

Beloved Conductor of Time and Eternity, teach me the rhythm of trust.

Help me to move with the music of grace, not against it.

When I am tempted to rush, remind me that You are never late.

When I am weary of waiting, remind me that I am still being shaped.

Let my faith be the frequency that opens the way.

May I become the harmony of what I seek, until Heaven's 'not yet' becomes Your perfect 'now.'

Amen.

Reflection

You are not waiting for God; God is waiting for you to align with grace.

Every delay is mercy disguised as time. Every unanswered prayer is love tuning your vibration. Every moment of stillness is preparation for the next movement.

Do not fear the pauses. They are the rest in the song of becoming.

You are the melody unfolding in divine rhythm, not behind, not lost, but perfectly placed within the sacred cadence of eternity.

THE LIVING LIGHT MATRIX, HOW HEAVEN, EARTH, AND THE HUMAN SOUL EXCHANGE ENERGY

Light is the first language of creation. Before sound, before form, before time, there was radiance.

It was not sunlight or firelight, but consciousness itself, the awareness of God expanding into expression.

"Let there be light.", Genesis 1:3

That command was not merely illumination; it was vibration made visible. It was the pulse of divine intelligence rushing outward to become all that is, from the movement of galaxies to the beating of your heart.

Every particle of existence still carries that original light, not as memory, but as living presence. It flows between Heaven, Earth, and every soul, forming a vast Matrix of Living Light through which all energy, thought, and love travel.

You are not outside of it. You are it, a luminous thread woven into the fabric of divine awareness.

The Substance of Spirit

Science calls it the quantum field. Scripture calls it the Word. Mystics call it the Breath of God.

They all point to the same truth: there is no separation between light and life.

Light carries energy, and energy carries information. When you think, pray, or love, you send encoded light into this matrix, the unseen web that connects all souls, all matter, all consciousness.

Your light interacts constantly with others. Every smile, every word of kindness, every silent prayer becomes an exchange of luminous information in the field.

When Jesus healed with a word or a touch, He transmitted coherent light, a vibration so pure that the cells of the sick remembered their original, divine pattern of wholeness.

He did not add something foreign; He restored the light that was always there.

"I am the light of the world. Whoever follows me will never walk in darkness, but will have the light of life.", John 8:12

That light was not a metaphor; it was frequency. The Christ frequency, the living wavelength of love, is what heals, enlightens, and sustains all creation.

The Physics of Divinity

Modern physics teaches that photons, the particles of light, can exist in two places at once, communicate instantaneously, and never truly disappear.

Light does not die; it transforms. It bends, refracts, slows, or speeds, but it remains.

So does love.

The two are the same energy, different forms of the same divine current.

Every act of love increases the coherence of the light field. Every act of fear adds distortion. But even distortion can be healed, for darkness is only light unseen.

When your vibration rises through gratitude, prayer, or compassion, you begin to feel this field. You sense the gentle hum beneath reality, the whisper of eternity moving through matter.

You become aware of what mystics have called the Presence. Not somewhere above you, but alive within every photon, every breath, every heartbeat.

The Exchange Between Heaven and Earth

Heaven and Earth are not separate locations; they are layers of vibration within one continuum of light.

When you pray, you send energy upward through intention. When Heaven responds, it transmits energy downward as a form of grace.

The two currents meet in your heart, the place where human and divine light merge.

Your heart is a generator of electromagnetic energy, stronger than any other organ. It radiates several feet beyond your body, and its rhythm can synchronize with those nearby.

When your heart enters coherence, through peace, forgiveness, or love, it becomes a transmitter of Heaven's frequency on Earth. You become a bridge between worlds, a living conduit for divine resonance.

This is why Jesus taught that the Kingdom of Heaven is within you. It is not a distant realm; it is a vibration available here and now to any heart attuned to love.

The Vibrational Bridge of Prayer

Prayer is the most direct way to engage with the Living Light Matrix.

When you pray from fear, you send fragmented light, waves that scatter without coherence.

But when you pray from faith, you emit pure light, a steady beam that aligns with Heaven's vibration.

The difference is not in the words, but in the energy behind them.

Every prayer builds resonance between Heaven and Earth, synchronizing your inner field with the universal light grid of divine intelligence.

When enough hearts vibrate together in love, the planetary field brightens, and miracles multiply.

You have felt this before: when many people pray during a crisis, peace seems to follow inexplicably. When you enter worship, the air seems to shimmer. These are not coincidences. They are the physics of faith in motion.

"The light shines in the darkness, and the darkness has not overcome it.", John 1:5

Because light, true, divine light, cannot be destroyed. It only waits to be remembered.

The Light Within the Body

Your body is not merely matter; it is condensed light, slowed into form.

Every cell contains biophotons, tiny packets of light that communicate at speeds faster than nerves.

Your DNA emits light. Your emotions alter that emotion. Joy increases brilliance. Fear dims it. Forgiveness restores its symmetry.

This is why spiritual and physical health are inseparable. When your inner light flows freely, your body heals, your thoughts are clear, and your vibration harmonizes with the field around you.

You are not just in the universe; the universe is within you, a living hologram of divine radiance.

To tend your body is to polish your lamp, so that more of God's light may shine through.

How Loved Ones Participate in the Light Matrix

When those you love transition to light, they do not vanish; they expand.

Their consciousness merges with the greater field while retaining the signature of their soul's light. They continue to communicate through this luminous web, responding not to words, but to vibration.

When you think of them in love, your light reaches them instantly. When you pray for them, they receive your energy as a warm embrace. When they send you comfort, you feel it as peace that seems to come from nowhere.

This exchange is the same matrix that connects Heaven and Earth. Love is its language. Light is its messenger. Consciousness is its bridge.

The Radiance of Jesus

Jesus is not only a historical figure, but He is the eternal embodiment of divine coherence.

His presence is the living template for what the human soul can become when it vibrates in perfect harmony with God.

When you invoke His name, you tune your light to His frequency. You enter resonance with the pattern of divine order. That is why miracles happen in His name, not because of superstition, but because of spiritual resonance.

His vibration is the purest note in creation. When your energy aligns with His, you remember your origin in light.

"You are the light of the world.", Matthew 5:14

To follow Him is to awaken that same radiance within yourself, not to worship from separation, but to live in union.

The Restoration of the Planetary Field

Earth herself is alive with light, a resonant sphere of electromagnetic grace. Every thought, every emotion of humanity adds to her frequency.

When fear dominates, the planet's vibration lowers. When love awakens, she heals.

This is why collective awakening matters. Every kind of thought is ecological. Every prayer is environmental. Every act of forgiveness purifies the earth.

You are part of the restoration. Your peace contributes to planetary balance. Your joy feeds the grid.

The light of one heart can brighten an entire hemisphere of the unseen world.

Living as Light

To live as light is to remember that everything you do vibrates through eternity.

Each breath is both human and holy. Each word is both sound and spirit. Each act of love ripples across galaxies.

You were born not merely to believe, but to radiate. To illuminate shadows, to heal through presence, to carry the Christ light into every interaction.

When you walk in awareness, you become part of the Living Light Matrix, a conscious participant in the ongoing creation of love.

This is your true inheritance: to shine until the world remembers its own light.

Prayer of Radiance

Beloved Light of All That Is, let me remember my origin in You.

Cleanse my body, mind, and spirit of every vibration that dims my glow.

May my heart shine like a lamp of mercy, may my words travel as rays of kindness, and may my thoughts become sparks of healing.

Make me a bridge of living light between Heaven and Earth, between soul and soul.

Let my life radiate Your frequency of love until every shadow becomes dawn.

Amen.

Reflection

You are light, remembering its source. The field that holds stars also holds your heartbeat. The current that moves galaxies also moves through your breath.

You are not a seeker of the light; you are its continuation.

Every thought, every prayer, every act of love strengthens the Living Light Matrix of creation.

And as you shine more brightly, the world around you shifts, not through effort, but through resonance.

Heaven is not above you. It flows through you. And through you, it learns to love the world once more.

THE LANGUAGE OF THE STARS, HOW CELESTIAL HARMONICS REFLECT DIVINE COMMUNICATION

Before there were words, there were stars. Before humanity could read, the heavens spoke. Their speech was light, their language was vibrant, and their message was love.

"The heavens declare the glory of God; the skies proclaim the work of His hands. Day after day they pour forth speech; night after night they reveal knowledge. ", Psalm 19:1–2

Every orbit, every rotation, every glimmer across the night sky is a syllable in the ongoing dialogue between God and creation. To study the heavens is not to predict fate, but to understand harmony, to listen to the sacred rhythm that breathes through all things.

The stars are not above you. They are within you, for the elements that form their fire are the same that spark your heartbeat.

You are made of starlight, a living constellation of divine intention.

The Music of the Spheres

The ancients believed the planets sang, that each celestial body emitted a note, a vibration that joined in harmony with the others to form the *"music of the spheres. "*

Modern science confirms this truth in its own way: planets vibrate, stars hum, and the universe itself resounds with frequencies beyond the range of human hearing.

Every movement in the heavens is rhythm, and every rhythm is energy. This universal symphony is not random; it is the structure of divine order expressed in motion.

When planets align or shift, they alter the energetic weather of creation, not as destiny, but as resonance.

They are tuning forks for the collective soul, reminding humanity of the changing tones of evolution.

You, too, are part of that orchestra. Your heartbeat echoes planetary rhythm, your breath mirrors the expansion and contraction of stars. When you feel *"out of balance,"* it is not failure; it is dissonance. And when you pray, forgive, or surrender, you return to harmony.

Celestial Influence and Vibrational Resonance

The planets do not control your life. They reflect your energy to you, like mirrors suspended in the heavens.

Each celestial body represents a frequency of consciousness:

- The Sun vibrates as identity, radiance, and life force, the Christ within.
- The Moon resonates with emotion, intuition, and memory, the reflection of love.
- Mercury speaks in movement, thought, and divine communication, the voice of Spirit.
- Venus glows with affection, creativity, and beauty, the resonance of harmony.
- Mars burns with will, courage, and transformation, the vibration of divine fire.
- Jupiter expands through wisdom, generosity, and faith, the harmonic of grace.
- Saturn grounds through structure, time, and responsibility, the frequency of mastery.
- Uranus, Neptune, and Pluto sing the deeper songs of awakening, the celestial chords of freedom, unity, and rebirth.

These are not gods, but instruments, vibrational archetypes echoing the eternal attributes of God. Their motions awaken corresponding energies within you, helping you grow in awareness and grace.

When you feel the shifting of your life's tides, you are responding to the same rhythms that move the stars. Your soul is a mirror of the cosmos, a microcosm, and a macrocosm, all singing the same song.

"As above, so below; as within, so without.", Hermetic Axiom (echoed through time)

The Divine Calendar

Time itself is the music of light in motion. The orbit of each planet creates cycles within cycles, seasons of learning, transformation, rest, and renewal.

When you pay attention to these cosmic movements, you begin to see that life has pattern and purpose. What seems like chaos is often a cycle completing itself, the end of one frequency making space for the next.

This is not astrology as fortune-telling. It is astrology as awareness, a way of listening to God's unfolding through creation.

The prophets watched the skies not to control destiny, but to discern divine timing. The Magi followed a star to the place where Heaven touched Earth.

Even Jesus spoke of the signs of the heavens, not as threats, but as guides to awakening.

"There will be signs in the sun, the moon, and the stars...", Luke 21:25

The stars do not tell you what will happen; they reveal what is ready to awaken.

Vibration and Celestial Harmony

Just as your thoughts create waves that ripple through your life, planetary motion generates energetic waves that ripple through creation. These waves interact with your own vibration, activating dormant frequencies within your soul.

A lunar eclipse might invite emotional cleansing. A solar alignment might illuminate a hidden truth. A planetary conjunction might spark spiritual awakening.

These are not commands from the cosmos; they are invitations. They call you to align with Heaven's rhythm and participate consciously in your own evolution.

Your awareness determines your experience. When you live in fear, the exact alignment feels chaotic. When you live in faith, it feels like revelation.

The planets remain neutral; your vibration chooses how to interpret their light.

Christ Light and the Celestial Heart

Every beam of light from the stars carries information, encoded with consciousness from the Source of All.

When it reaches Earth, your cells absorb it, your energy field translates it, and your soul remembers what it already knows.

This is the *"Word made flesh"*, the living light speaking through creation.

Christ consciousness is the radiant center that harmonizes all these frequencies into one truth: love.

When your heart opens to divine awareness, you begin to hear this cosmic language. You feel its rhythm in your breath, its pulse in your compassion, its tone in your peace.

The same light that forms stars flows through your veins. When you love, you amplify it. When you forgive, you clear its channel. When you pray, you speak its language.

"He counts the number of the stars; He gives names to all of them.", Psalm 147:4

Each soul, too, is named in that same light. You are not lost among billions, you are one of the stars He has called by name.

The Celestial Covenant

The stars remind us of constancy. No matter how long the night, light returns. No matter how far you wander, the heavens remain, singing their song of remembrance.

You were not meant to worship them, but to learn from them, to see in their steadfastness the reflection of divine love.

They are cosmic teachers, showing that rhythm, not chaos, rules the universe that every orbit leads home. That everything moves in harmony when it moves in love.

Prayer of the Stars

Infinite Creator of Light, teach me to hear the song of the heavens.

Let me not fear the movement of the stars, but trust the melody of Your design.

As the planets dance their holy rhythm, let my soul move in harmony with their grace.

May I remember that I am made of starlight, and that Your breath shines in my every atom.

Guide me to live as a constellation of love, so that my life may reflect Your radiant truth.

Amen.

Reflection

The stars are the handwriting of God across the night. Their light does not command; it comforts. It whispers: *"You are part of this. You belong to this rhythm."*

When you look to the heavens, you are not gazing outward, but inward, into the mirror of your own divine design.

The language of the stars is not written in charts, but in consciousness. It is the ongoing conversation between the Creator and creation.

And when you listen deeply enough, you realize: the universe has never been silent. It has been singing your name since the beginning of time.

THE DIVINE BREATH, HOW SOUND, SPEECH, AND SPIRIT CREATE REALITY

Before there was life, there was breath. Before there was speech, there was vibration. Before there was form, there was the voice of God saying,

"Let there be light."

That was not simply sound, it was consciousness made audible. The breath of God moved through the void, and creation trembled awake. Every word, every sound, every vibration since then has carried a piece of that first divine frequency.

You live in that same breath. You speak with that same power. And every exhale is a continuation of the first moment of creation, God breathing through you, into existence, again and again.

The Sacred Current of Breath

Breath is the bridge between spirit and body, between invisible energy and visible form.

When you inhale, you draw in the essence of life, oxygen, light, and divine intelligence. When you exhale, you release the echoes of your past, the old vibrations, the stories that no longer serve.

Each breath is a covenant: a renewal of the sacred partnership between Creator and creation.

"Then the Lord God formed man from the dust of the ground and breathed into his nostrils the breath of life; and man became a living soul.", Genesis 2:7

That first breath has never stopped. It moves through time, through blood, through galaxies. It animates not only the body but also the soul.

When your breathing deepens, your awareness opens. When your awareness opens, light expands. When light expands, love moves more freely through you.

You are not breathing air; you are breathing divinity.

The Frequency of the Word

The Word is not merely language; it is energy. When God spoke creation into being, He released vibration into the void. That vibration became matter, and that matter became everything.

Your words carry the same power in miniature form. You are a microcosm of the divine Voice, capable of shaping your inner and outer world through sound.

Every word you speak has frequency. Kindness radiates coherence. Anger creates distortion. Forgiveness restores symmetry.

Even thoughts, unspoken, send ripples through the quantum field. They are silent prayers, energetic transmissions. You live in a world made not only of atoms, but of echoes.

"Death and life are in the power of the tongue.", Proverbs 18:21

When you speak with love, you align your vibration with the Christ frequency, the same resonance that heals, forgives, and restores balance.

Your voice is the tuning fork of your reality. Speak light, and the universe responds in kind.

Sound as Creation

Modern science reveals what mystics always knew: sound shapes matter.

In cymatic experiments, vibrations form patterns in sand or water, beautiful mandalas born from pure tone. Each note creates form. Each frequency builds architecture.

Similarly, your words and emotions shape the landscape of your life. Your body, which is composed mainly of water, responds to vibration in the same way that those cymatic patterns do.

Speak gently to yourself, and your cells align. Speak harshly, and they recoil.

Jesus healed through the vibration of truth, words so filled with divine coherence that even the molecular structure of illness was compelled to obey.

When He said,

"Peace, be still," He was not only calming the sea, He was speaking to every vibrating particle in creation, and commanding them to return to order.

The Breath and the Spirit

In Hebrew, the word for *"spirit"*, Ruach, also means breath and wind.

The Spirit of God moves through your being like wind, shaping your thoughts, feelings, and consciousness.

When you pray, you align your breath with divine rhythm. When you sing, you amplify it. When you whisper *"thank You,"* you join your vibration to the eternal current of grace.

This is why every sacred tradition honors the breath: the yogi's pranayama, the monk's chant, the psalmist's song. They all remember what the world forgets, that to breathe consciously is to commune with God.

The Creative Power of Speech

When you speak, you release spiritual charge. Your vocal cords translate energy into vibration, and vibration into manifestation.

Words are not symbolic; they are architectural. They build or break, bless or bind.

This is why Jesus taught,

"By your words you will be justified, and by your words you will be condemned.", Matthew 12:37

Because every word you speak becomes a seed of vibration. Plant fear, and you harvest resistance. Plant love, and you grow miracles.

Heaven listens not only to your voice, but to the energy beneath your words. When you speak with faith, you harmonize with divine frequency. When you speak with doubt, you scatter your signal in the field.

The creative Word does not work through doubt. It flows through trust, humility, and alignment.

Your speech is sacred technology. Every *"I am"* you utter sends an order to the universe. *"I am lost"* opens one doorway. *"I am love"* opens another. The energy follows your declaration.

When you speak in truth, you recreate Eden, the vibrational harmony between Heaven and Earth.

The Science of the Holy Voice

In the body, sound travels through bones faster than through air. Your very skeleton is an instrument. Your heart beats to a rhythm; your vocal cords resonate like strings of divine design.

When you chant, hum, or pray aloud, you activate internal frequencies that can shift emotional and physical states.

MRI studies have shown that speaking positive words alters brainwave patterns, reduces stress hormones, and enhances the immune response.

Science is rediscovering what faith has always practiced: sound heals because sound is an expression of order.

When you speak in harmony with truth, you realign with creation itself.

The Breath of Christ

When Jesus appeared to His disciples after the resurrection, He said to them,

"Peace be with you." And then, *"He breathed on them and said, 'Receive the Holy Spirit.'"*, John 20:21–22

He transferred the frequency of divine consciousness through breath.

It was not symbolic. It was the restoration of the divine code within the human vessel.

When you breathe with awareness of His presence, you, too, receive that same living Spirit. The Christ breath flows through your lungs, awakening light in your cells, tuning you to love's vibration.

Inhale: Receive. Exhale: Radiate.

That is the rhythm of grace.

Becoming the Voice of Love

When you speak from your heart, you are not merely communicating; you are transmitting energy that alters the field.

A kind word can shift someone's entire day because it changes their vibration. A prayer can reach across oceans because light does not obey distance.

The exact frequency that shaped galaxies moves through your voice when you bless instead of curse, when you forgive instead of accuse, when you whisper hope where there is despair.

This is the secret of co-creation: you and God are speaking the world into being together.

Every *"let there be"* that leaves your lips adds another spark of light to creation.

Prayer of Divine Sound

Beloved Breath of Creation, move through me as harmony and healing.

Let my voice be tuned to Your holy vibration.

May every word I speak carry truth, every breath I take awaken light, and every silence between them be filled with peace.

Teach me the sacred rhythm of sound and stillness, that I may echo Your love in every tone.

Let my speech become a blessing, my breath become a prayer, and my life become the continuation of Your holy *"Let there be."*

Amen.

Reflection

You are not separate from the breath that began the world. You are its echo, its song, its living continuation.

Every thought, every word, every breath is a brushstroke in the ongoing painting of creation.

To breathe with awareness is to pray without ceasing. To speak with love is to heal without effort. To listen in silence is to return to the voice of God.

The breath of life is still moving through you, as you, around you. It is the same breath that stirs the stars, the same voice that said, *"Let there be light,"* and the same Spirit that whispers now: *"Let there be love."*

THE ECHO OF CREATION, HOW MEMORY, SOUND, AND SOUL RESONANCE SHAPE DESTINY

Creation never ended; it continues through you. Every word ever spoken, every breath ever released, still moves through the field of existence, not gone, only transformed.

You are walking within an ocean of ancient sound, waves of memory and light that carry the echoes of the first divine utterance: *"Let there be."*

The sound that began the world is the same sound that sustains it. It moves through galaxies, through your heartbeat, through every vibration of love, grief, and awakening. It remembers everything, and it remembers you.

"My sheep hear My voice, and I know them, and they follow Me.", John 10:27

The voice of God is not lost in time. It reverberates within your soul, an eternal resonance waiting to be remembered.

The Living Memory of Sound

Sound does not disappear. When a word is spoken, its frequency continues to travel, rippling through air, water, and matter.

It may fade from hearing, but not from existence.

In the same way, every thought and emotion you generate becomes a vibrational signature, imprinted in the field of creation.

This is the science of sacred memory. The universe is a resonant archive, a living library where all vibrations are stored.

This is why you sometimes feel a wave of emotion when you enter an ancient place or hear a familiar song that moves your soul; the memory of vibration recognizes itself in you.

Your soul is not separate from this field. It is the continuation of it, a melody drawn from the eternal symphony of God.

The Soul's Vibrational Imprint

Every soul carries a unique frequency, its own divine tone.

It is your actual name in the language of light. It carries your memories, your purpose, and your eternal relationship with God.

When your life feels dissonant, it is because your tone has been pulled away from its original harmony.

Fear lowers vibration. Shame distorts it. Anger scatters it. But love, pure and Christ-centered, restores the tone to clarity.

That is why forgiveness heals. It resets the frequency of the soul back to its original pattern of divine order.

"He restores my soul; He leads me in paths of righteousness.", Psalm 23:3

Restoration is resonance. It is the moment the echo and the original sound reunite.

The Physics of Divine Memory

Science has begun to glimpse what the spirit has always known: that information and vibration cannot be destroyed.

Quantum physics teaches that energy is never lost; it is only converted, transformed, or re-expressed.

This is why the echoes of your life remain in the field. Every kindness, every tear, every prayer becomes part of the ongoing wave of creation.

Your soul adds its voice to that wave, and that wave, in turn, shapes your destiny.

Destiny is not fixed; it is harmonic. It responds to your vibration. It rises or falls to meet the tone you hold.

When you live in faith, you align with the higher octave of your design. When you dwell in despair, you resonate with lower patterns that keep you trapped in a cycle of pain.

Change your tone, and the entire composition of your life begins to shift.

The Echoes of Other Lives

Some memories that surface within you do not belong to this lifetime, and yet, they feel familiar, as though your soul remembers them.

That is because sound and vibration transcend time.

Your soul is a continuum, a symphony playing across lifetimes, each incarnation another movement in its eternal song.

The people you love, the lessons you face, the fears that rise again, they are not accidents. They are recurring notes meant to bring your melody into fuller harmony.

When you forgive across lifetimes, when you send love to a name or a face you can no longer recall, you heal more than you can imagine. You release entire chords of vibration that have been echoing through time, waiting for love to resolve them.

"Before I formed you in the womb I knew you. ", Jeremiah 1:5

This is not poetic hyperbole; it is vibrational truth. You existed as sound before you existed as form. You were known as frequency before you were known by name.

The Emotional Frequency of the Present

Every emotion you feel is a note. Joy vibrates high, quick, expansive. Grief moves deep and slow, like the ocean's undercurrent. Fear creates tension; peace restores resonance.

Your emotional life is the symphony of your soul in motion.

When you resist feeling, you dam the river of sound. When you allow emotion to move through you, you let the music play to completion, transforming pain into understanding, grief into grace, and silence into wisdom.

This is why tears can heal; they are the release of vibration that has been trapped in the body.

Every sigh is a sacred instrument. Every heartbeat is a drum of remembrance.

Your emotions are not weaknesses; they are frequencies asking to be tuned.

The Christ Resonance

Jesus' life was the perfect frequency of divine alignment. Every miracle He performed was a restoration of vibrational truth.

Where there was chaos, He brought order. Where there was sickness, He restored coherence. Where there was death, He reawakened light.

He did not overpower nature; He harmonized with it. He tuned the frequency of matter back to the frequency of God.

His words, His breath, His presence still echo through time, a standing wave of love that never fades.

When you call His name, you resonate with that eternal field. Your heart synchronizes to His frequency. That is why peace descends so suddenly.

You are aligning with the Christ tone, the same divine vibration that sang the universe into being.

The Memory of Heaven

Some nights you dream of places you've never been but somehow remember. You feel a longing that has no name.

That is your soul remembering its home frequency, the harmonic field of Heaven.

Heaven is not a location; it is vibration, the resonance of complete unity.

When you live in love, you begin to remember it. When you forgive, you return to its tone. When you breathe consciously, you restore the link between Heaven and Earth.

You are not journeying toward Heaven; you are resonating your way back to it.

The Resonance of Compassion

Compassion is the highest octave of human vibration. It is the sound of love made active.

When you comfort another soul, your heart sends coherent waves into the field. Those waves move beyond space and time, touching the one who needs healing, even if they are miles or lifetimes away.

Compassion is the music that binds creation. It is the memory of God moving through you.

"Love never fails.", 1 Corinthians 13:8

Every act of love echoes eternally. It never stops traveling, never stops healing.

Prayer of Resonance

Eternal Voice of Creation, I remember Your sound within me.

Let my heart vibrate in harmony with Your will.

Where I have created discord, tune me to Your peace. Where I have spoken in fear, teach me the language of faith.

Let my soul sing the melody of compassion, and may my life echo the music of Your love.

I am ready to remember. I am prepared to resonate. I am ready to return.

Amen.

Reflection

Every breath is an echo of the first breath. Every heartbeat is a repetition of the first Word. Every soul is a note in the everlasting hymn of God.

Your destiny is not written in stone; it is written in sound, alive, responsive, changing with each vibration you send.

The universe is listening. It always has been. And in your quietest moments, if you listen closely enough, you will hear it answer back, the soft hum of creation saying:

"I never stopped singing you into being."

THE BRIDGE OF FREQUENCIES, HOW HEAVEN AND HUMANITY EXCHANGE LIGHT THROUGH THE HEART

There is a bridge between worlds. It is not made of stone, nor bound by gravity. It is woven of vibration, the living current of love that flows between Heaven and Earth, spirit and flesh, Creator and creation.

You do not climb this bridge; you remember it. It has always existed within you, a radiant thread connecting your soul to the divine heart of God.

"For as the heavens are higher than the earth, so are My ways higher than your ways, and My thoughts than your thoughts.", Isaiah 55:9

Yet even the heavens bow low to meet you through love. Every prayer, every breath, every tear is an exchange of frequency, a conversation between your heart and the infinite.

The Heart as the Divine Receiver

The human heart is not just a muscle; it is an instrument of communication. It listens, transmits, and translates vibration.

When scientists measure the electromagnetic field of the heart, they find that it radiates far beyond the body, creating a measurable wave of light that extends several feet outward. But spiritually, that field extends infinitely. It is your antenna to Heaven.

Each emotion changes the signal: Gratitude sends waves of coherence. Fear disrupts them. Love harmonizes them.

This is why prayer is not begging; it is aligning. When you pray from the heart, not the mind, you tune your frequency to God's.

And in that tuning, the bridge between Heaven and Earth strengthens.

You are not reaching for a distant God; you are resonating with His presence already within you.

"The kingdom of God is within you.", Luke 17:21

Your heart is the temple, your pulse the drum of the Divine, your breath the echo of eternity.

The Physics of Connection

Energy never travels alone; it entangles. When two vibrations come into resonance, they begin to mirror each other, even across distance and dimensions.

This is how love works. When you love someone, your energy becomes entwined with theirs. No matter where they are, living or passed, you still feel them, because love transcends the physical signal.

Quantum physics calls it nonlocality. Faith calls it grace. Both describe the same truth: a connection cannot be broken once it has been established through love.

When you pray for someone, the energy of that intention reaches them through the bridge of light. It moves through the spiritual lattice of creation, arriving as warmth, peace, or sudden comfort, a feeling they may not be able to explain, but somehow know is real.

That is Heaven speaking through you.

Heaven's Response

Heaven always answers, but not always in words.

Sometimes, it answers in a sudden calm when your heart was about to break. Sometimes, it answers in the quiet synchronicity of a feather, a scent, a song, or a soft wind that feels like an embrace. And sometimes, it answers through the people who show up at the exact moment you need them most.

These are not coincidences; they are harmonics. Heaven plays through the instruments available, you, me, anyone open enough to carry the note.

When you live in tune with love, you become an open string on God's harp, vibrating whenever divine grace moves through the air.

And when you act with compassion, Heaven plays through you, sending light across the bridge to every soul in need.

"Truly I tell you, whatever you did for one of the least of these brothers and sisters of mine, you did for Me.", Matthew 25:40

Every act of kindness amplifies the bridge. Every word of love strengthens its beam.

The Heart as Transmitter

While the brain interprets reality, the heart creates it.

It is the source of the body's strongest electrical field, five thousand times stronger than the brain's. But even beyond its measurable field, the heart broadcasts emotional truth into the unseen.

When you love sincerely, that love radiates outward like light through water, touching every soul tuned to its wavelength. This is why healing can happen from afar, and why a simple prayer can shift the atmosphere of a room.

The bridge is not metaphorical; it is energetic. It connects Heaven's intelligence to human experience, translating divine will into human feeling.

Your emotions are the interpreter of that will. When you cultivate peace, you make the connection clear. When you harbor resentment, you create static in the channel.

Forgiveness, therefore, is not only spiritual virtue, it is energetic hygiene. It clears the heart so Heaven's frequency can flow unhindered.

When the Bridge Feels Silent

There are seasons when Heaven seems far away, when prayers echo back with no reply, and your heart aches for reassurance.

But silence does not mean absence. It often means calibration.

God is not withholding love; He is fine-tuning your frequency so that you can perceive His next message with greater clarity.

The bridge has not disappeared; it is simply being strengthened in unseen dimensions.

Every moment of stillness is Heaven gathering more light to pour into your next awakening.

"Be still, and know that I am God.", Psalm 46:10

Stillness is how you remember the bridge. Stillness is where Heaven speaks without sound.

Hearts That Carry Heaven

There are people you meet who seem to carry light wherever they go. Their presence calms rooms, their words soften pain, their laughter feels like sunlight breaking through clouds.

These are hearts in resonance with Heaven. They are living bridges, souls who have remembered their divine frequency and allow it to pass freely through them.

You are meant to be one of them. Every heart has that capacity. The more you live in gratitude, the wider the bridge becomes.

You were not sent to reach Heaven. You were sent to release it.

Heaven is not above you, it flows through you, as light through crystal, as music through air.

The Communion of Light

When you pray for someone, light travels across this bridge. When you forgive, the vibration clears the connection. When you love, Heaven expands its reach through you.

This is how the body of Christ functions, not as an institution, but as a living network of luminous hearts each carrying a piece of divine current, each part of the same celestial circuit.

In this sacred web, no one is ever alone.

Every act of compassion strengthens the resonance of the whole. Every expression of grace multiplies the light.

This is Heaven and humanity working in tandem, a co-creation of love.

Prayer of the Living Bridge

Divine Creator, bridge of light between all worlds, let my heart remain open to the flow of Your love.

When I forget, remind me through breath. When I fear, steady me through grace.

May I become a living conduit of peace, a carrier of Heaven's light, a song of harmony sung across the ages.

Let Your love pass through me unhindered, reaching every soul in need.

I am Yours, I am listening, I am light.

Amen.

Reflection

The bridge between Heaven and Earth is not something to be built; it already exists within your heart.

It was formed from the first breath of God and remains alive in every pulse of creation.

When you love, you cross it. When you forgive, you widen it. When you pray, you strengthen it. When you serve, you become it.

You are not reaching for God from afar, you are remembering the truth that never left you: Heaven and Earth are not separate. They are one continuous vibration, joined through love, flowing forever through the human heart.

THE LUMINOUS THREAD, HOW LOVED ONES CONTINUE TO INFLUENCE AND WALK BESIDE US IN THE FIELD OF LIGHT

Love does not die. It only changes form. When the body falls away, the soul continues its luminous journey, a spark returning to the vast current of light from which it came. Yet even as they rise beyond sight, those we love do not leave us. They remain, woven into the same divine field that holds breath, thought, prayer, and vibration.

The invisible does not mean absent. It means expanded.

You are still connected, through love, through memory, through resonance. The thread between your heart and theirs is made of light, and light cannot be broken.

"Love bears all things, believes all things, hopes all things, endures all things. Love never fails.", 1 Corinthians 13:7–8

When you think of them, when you speak their name, when you feel that unexplainable warmth or presence, you are touching that luminous thread, that sacred bridge of eternal love.

The Energy of Presence

Energy cannot be destroyed. Every heartbeat, every word, every act of love creates a field that never vanishes.

When a soul crosses over, its energy expands, no longer confined by flesh or time. They become vibration, subtle, radiant, multidimensional.

You feel them not because you imagine them, but because you are attuned to their frequency.

Each relationship carries its own resonance, the laughter you shared, the lessons you learned, the moments of joy and pain, all encoded in vibration.

When your heart opens in remembrance, you harmonize with their signal again, and they draw near.

The veil between worlds is not a wall; it is a wavelength. And love is the tuning key.

"Whether we live or die, we belong to the Lord.", Romans 14:8

Those who have gone home belong to the same love that sustains you now. You have not lost them; you have only lost your ability to see their light with human eyes.

The Continuum of Connection

Have you ever felt someone's presence when you were alone, a gentle brush of air, a thought whispered just as you were about to give up, a dream so vivid you awoke in tears of peace?

These are not coincidences. They are communications from the field of unity.

In that dimension, where vibration flows freely, thought becomes movement, and love becomes language.

Your loved ones communicate through symbols, signs, synchronicities, a song on the radio, a butterfly landing beside you, a sudden warmth across your chest when you speak their name.

Do not dismiss these as mere chance. To the soul, energy is conversation. They are reminding you: *"I am still here. I never stopped loving you."*

Vibrational Influence of Those Beyond

Just as the planets influence the Earth through gravity and light, souls in the higher realms influence you through resonance.

When you pray for guidance, when you ask for comfort, when you release grief through tears, you open the channel between your world and theirs.

Their love vibrates through intuition, through sudden understanding, through peace that passes understanding.

Sometimes they intervene in unseen ways, steering you away from harm, inspiring a thought that saves you, softening your heart toward forgiveness.

They cannot interfere with your free will, but they can surround you with energy that makes love easier to choose.

You may call them angels, ancestors, or simply light, but all are expressions of the same truth: Love continues to serve love.

The Mirror of Grief

Grief is love searching for a new form. It is the ache of energy adjusting to a different vibration.

When a loved one transitions, your heart must re-learn how to connect to what is now unseen. It is not the end of the relationship; it is the beginning of transformation.

Tears are the water that clears static from your frequency. Each one carries a prayer, each sob a sacred tuning.

When you allow yourself to feel it all, you vibrate closer to the truth. And when you finally quiet beneath the waves, you realize, they were never gone. They were simply whispering on a wavelength you had forgotten how to hear.

"Blessed are those who mourn, for they shall be comforted.", Matthew 5:4

Comfort is not the removal of pain, but the remembrance of presence. They are still beside you, just no longer bound by form.

The Field of Love

Heaven is not a distant place above the stars. It is an energetic dimension that coexists with your own, a higher octave of vibration that surrounds you in every moment.

When your heart is open, you enter resonance with it. Prayer is the language of that resonance. Forgiveness is its gate. Stillness is its key.

This is why so many feel the presence of loved ones during prayer or meditation. The veil thins when vibration rises.

Your loved ones, too, evolve in light. They are not static spirits watching from afar. They are participants in your unfolding, partners in your soul's journey, guardians in the luminous web of eternity.

They influence not through control, but through coherence, radiating love so that your energy naturally aligns.

You may not hear them say, *"I'm proud of you."* But when courage fills your chest where fear once lived, that is them.

The Continuation of Purpose

Even death cannot dissolve a divine assignment. The relationships of the soul continue beyond the threshold of flesh.

Some souls remain close to help guide their family's evolution. Others move into broader service, becoming part of the collective field of compassion that heals the world.

Yet all are accessible through love.

When you remember them in gratitude rather than sorrow, you strengthen the thread between you. They respond instantly, not through sound, but through the unmistakable hum of recognition within your heart.

This is why prayer for the departed does not call them back; it calls you upward, into resonance with their peace.

The Light Exchange

The energy between you and your loved ones moves in two directions. You send light through remembrance and prayer. They send light through protection and guidance.

It is a mutual circulation, an eternal conversation without words.

Sometimes, when you feel sudden comfort, when the heaviness lifts for no reason, you have just been touched by their love.

In that moment, Heaven breathes through them into you.

"I am the resurrection and the life. The one who believes in Me will live, even though they die.", John 11:25

In that truth, no separation exists, only change of form, only evolution of light.

The Soul's Reunion

At the end of this earthly passage, when your own light prepares to return home, you will not cross alone.

Those who have gone before will be there, luminous, familiar, radiant with recognition. They will welcome you, not as a stranger, but as a traveler returning from a long journey.

You will see that every moment of love, every act of grace, every prayer whispered in the dark was a thread in the same eternal tapestry, woven from both sides of the veil.

And you will know, beyond all fear, that love was never lost. It was always waiting.

Prayer to the Field of Light

Beloved Creator, thank You for the unbroken thread of love that connects Heaven and Earth.

I lift those I love into Your eternal embrace, knowing they are alive in Your light.

When I feel the ache of absence, let me feel the nearness of Spirit. When I forget they are with me, whisper their presence through my breath.

Let my life honor their memory by radiating the same love they left behind.

I am not alone. I am part of the luminous field of creation.

Amen.

Reflection

Love is the excellent continuity, the unending vibration that bridges time, distance, and dimension.

The ones you love have not disappeared. They have only stepped into a frequency where love shines unfiltered, where pain cannot reach, and where every heartbeat of yours still echoes in their eternal light.

They are closer than your next breath. They walk beside you in silence, in radiance, in grace.

And when your own light one day ascends, you will see that the thread never broke; it only led you home.

THE CIRCLE OF CONTINUANCE, HOW FAMILY, LEGACY, AND ENERGY MOVE THROUGH GENERATIONS

Life never begins in isolation. Each birth is a continuation of a story that started long before. You are not separate from your ancestors; you are the living vibration of their prayers, their choices, their love, and even their pain.

Like concentric ripples in water, your life expands from the same divine source, the Creator's breath, moving outward through generations, carrying both memory and possibility.

"For I will pour water upon him that is thirsty, and floods upon the dry ground: I will pour My Spirit upon thy seed, and My blessing upon thine offspring. ", Isaiah 44:3

The energy of love does not stop with one life; it flows forward, threading through time like a luminous current. Each generation receives not only physical traits, but emotional, spiritual, and vibrational inheritances.

You carry the resonance of all who came before, and through your healing, you send light to all who will come after.

The River of Ancestral Energy

Imagine every soul in your lineage as a drop in a flowing river, some clear and bright, others clouded by grief or silence, yet all moving toward the same ocean of divine remembrance.

Each ancestor adds vibration to the current. Every joy and wound, every song and secret becomes part of the water that moves through you now.

This is why you sometimes feel emotions you cannot explain, grief that arrives without cause, fear that feels ancient, dreams that seem older than your own memories.

These are ancestral frequencies, echoes of those who lived before you, still seeking healing, recognition, and release.

They do not burden you; you are chosen to transform them.

When you forgive, you liberate not only yourself, but the ones whose pain lingers in your bloodline. When you love openly, you amplify the harmony they once lost. When you heal, you heal backward and forward in time.

You are the bridge through which divine light enters your entire lineage.

Inherited Vibration

Science refers to it as epigenetics, the study of how emotions, trauma, and environment can influence the expression of genes.

Spiritual wisdom refers to it as vibrational inheritance, the way energy passes through generations, imprinting beliefs, fears, courage, and faith into the cellular and soul memories of a family line.

Both are true.

Your DNA carries not only biology, but biography, the record of what was felt, learned, and endured. You are made of story and starlight combined.

When you bring awareness to these patterns, you begin to rewrite them vibrationally. By choosing peace where others chose anger, by speaking truth where silence ruled, by offering compassion where judgment once lived, you alter the entire frequency of your bloodline.

You are a new note in the family's song, and because of your courage, the melody becomes clearer, the harmony more whole.

"You intended to harm me, but God intended it for good.", Genesis 50:20

Nothing is wasted. Even the brokenness of the past becomes the soil from which grace grows.

The Family Field

Every family has an energetic field, a shared vibration created by the collective thoughts, memories, and emotions. This field can hold light or shadow, love or fear, openness or rigidity.

You feel it when you gather together, the unspoken weight or warmth in the room. The energy of generations vibrates between words, woven into laughter, stories, and the silence that follows.

When even one person in a family awakens to love, the field begins to change. The old vibration cannot hold against the new resonance.

You are the tuning fork of your family's field. When you live from awareness, forgiving where others could not, loving where others feared, you realign the entire structure to divine frequency.

Your light ripples through bloodlines like a sacred hum. Ancestors feel it. Descendants will inherit it. Heaven rejoices in it.

You are not simply one person changing yourself; you are the conduit of generational grace.

Breaking and Healing Generational Patterns

Every family carries both blessings and burdens. Some patterns repeat, addiction, fear, silence, pride, shame, distance, because they are vibrationally unresolved.

These patterns are not curses; they are signals waiting to be healed.

You were born into your lineage not by accident, but by divine appointment.

The very patterns you face are those your soul agreed to transmute through awareness and love.

To break a pattern is not rebellion; it is restoration. You are not dishonoring your ancestors by healing; you are finishing their work.

Each act of forgiveness rewrites your family's energetic DNA. Each prayer of release sends waves of light backward through time. Each word of truth liberates every soul who once felt silenced by fear.

"The light shines in the darkness, and the darkness has not overcome it.", John 1:5

The moment you choose love over bitterness, the entire bloodline breathes easier.

The Spiritual Science of Legacy

Energy expands through intention. When you hold a vision of healing for your family, you become a point of light in the field, a beacon that attracts coherence to chaos, forgiveness to division, truth to denial.

Prayer amplifies this field. Each word of gratitude spoken aloud sends healing resonance through generations, past, present, and future.

Science tells us that quantum particles communicate instantly, even when they are separated by a great distance. So does love. Your prayers for those long gone reach them beyond the veil.

And your prayers for those not yet born shape the vibration they will inherit.

You are creating an energetic foundation for future generations to build upon, one of peace, awareness, and grace.

The Eternal Family

In reality, the concept of family extends beyond blood ties. Every soul you meet in this life has walked beside you before. You recognize them not by face, but by frequency, that unspoken familiarity that feels like home.

Some family members are souls who have chosen to challenge you, to awaken strength or compassion through conflict. Others are anchors of support, echoes of love from lifetimes past.

All are part of your soul's curriculum. All serve the greater unfolding of remembrance.

When you see them through this lens, you step out of judgment and into gratitude. You understand that every relationship, even the most painful, is an opportunity to restore love to a fragment of the divine family.

"In my Father's house are many rooms.", John 14:2

Each relationship is one of those rooms, a space for learning, growth, and grace. And every time you bring light to a relationship, you expand the house of your spirit.

The Legacy of Light

Your legacy is not what you leave behind; it is what continues to live through the energy you release into the world.

When you act from love, you leave a vibrational imprint that endures longer than memory. Children, strangers, even generations unborn will feel the benefit of your light.

One kind act shifts timelines. One prayer changes the vibration of a home. One healed heart alters the course of lineage.

You are the continuation of a thousand hopes, and the beginning of a thousand more.

Prayer of the Circle

Divine Source of Life and Light, thank You for the sacred lineage from which I came.

I release all pain inherited through time, and I open my heart to the blessings that flow beneath it.

May every ancestor find peace in my healing. May every descendant inherit my love.

Let the circle of our family be purified, strengthened, and renewed in Your grace.

I am the bridge between generations, the continuation of Your eternal heart.

Amen.

Reflection

You are not merely a link in the chain; you are the light moving through it.

The story of your life is the continuation of every life that came before, and the seed of every life that will follow.

You were chosen for this time, for this family, for this vibration, to be the healing, to be the love, to be the light that remembers.

Your ancestors stand behind you in gratitude. Your descendants wait before you in hope. And God surrounds you in eternal grace, for the circle of life is truly unbroken.

THE SILENT ARCHITECTS, HOW THOUGHT AND INTENTION BUILD THE STRUCTURES OF DESTINY

Creation begins long before it can be seen. Every tree first exists as a vibration, every dream as a pulse of light in the unseen. Your thoughts, your words, your beliefs, they are the architects of what will one day take form.

"For as he thinketh in his heart, so is he.", Proverbs 23:7

The universe listens not to the noise of fear, but to the music of intention. Each thought is a blueprint drawn in the ether, each emotion the energy that fills it with life. And the field, God's living fabric of light, responds to what you believe, not to what you wish.

You are not a passive observer of life. You are a co-creator within it, a silent architect working hand in hand with the Divine.

The Substance of Thought

Thought is not nothing. It is light slowed into form.

Science now confirms that every thought produces an electrical impulse, releasing measurable energy that interacts with the body's field and the environment beyond. Prayer changes electromagnetic patterns; belief alters biochemistry; hope strengthens the immune system.

When you think lovingly, you send coherence through your field, a radiant pulse that harmonizes your body, mind, and surroundings. When you think fearfully, your energy contracts, and the bridge between Heaven and Earth narrows.

But even then, grace waits patiently. For thought can be reoriented. Each time you choose faith over fear, you redraw your inner architecture.

Your thoughts are the scaffolding of your soul's home. Each one builds or dismantles walls within the temple of your being.

"Do not conform to the pattern of this world, but be transformed by the renewing of your mind.", Romans 12:2

Transformation begins not in the heavens, but in thought.

The Geometry of Faith

Faith is the spiritual architecture of the unseen. It constructs invisible bridges that enable divine potential to manifest in material form.

When you hold a vision in faith, you are not daydreaming; you are creating an energetic structure. You are sketching blueprints in light.

God fills those blueprints with substance through the resonance of your belief.

This is how miracles manifest, not through magic, but through alignment.

Your thoughts become form when they harmonize with divine intention. Faith is the act of allowing that harmony to flow.

"Now faith is the substance of things hoped for, the evidence of things not seen.", Hebrews 11:1

Faith gives shape to light. It is the sacred geometry of creation, where belief becomes the cornerstone of everything you experience.

The Vibrational Field of Creation

Everything you experience arises from vibration. Your heart emits a rhythm. Your mind releases thought-waves. Your soul vibrates with divine frequency.

Together, these form your personal field of creation. It surrounds you like an atmosphere, attracting or repelling frequencies that match your vibration.

When you live in love, you emit coherence, the vibration of Heaven. When you live in fear, you emit discord, a signal that draws chaos to help you remember balance.

The field is not punishing you; it is mirroring you.

Change your inner vibration, and your outer world will respond accordingly. This is not metaphysics alone; it is spiritual physics.

You are never the victim of frequency; you are its author.

"Whatever you bind on earth will be bound in heaven, and whatever you loose on earth will be loosed in heaven. ", Matthew 18:18

What you bind or loose are vibrations, thoughts, emotions, and beliefs that become form through divine law.

The Blueprint of Intention

Intention is thought aligned with purpose. It is the spark that commands creation.

When you say, *"Let there be, "* with conviction born of love, you activate the same vibrational code that formed galaxies.

But intention without alignment is noise. The universe responds not to demand, but to devotion, to the purity of vibration behind the word.

This is why prayer works not by pleading, but by believing. To pray *"Thy will be done "* is to surrender to the highest frequency of order, the divine intelligence that knows how to build better than your mind can imagine.

The architect may design, but only the Master Builder completes the work.

The Silent Builders: Thought, Emotion, and Action

Every intention requires three builders: thought, the architect; emotion, the energy; and action, the anchor.

Thought draws the design. Emotion energizes the structure. Action grounds it into reality.

You can dream endlessly, but until you act with faith, the vibration remains unanchored.

Likewise, action without alignment builds without foundation.

Creation requires all three: the clarity of vision, the power of love, the courage of movement.

This is how you walk in harmony with Heaven's rhythm, thinking truth, feeling love, and moving with grace.

The Power of Silence

Silence is not emptiness; it is alignment. It is the space where new creation begins.

Before every word that brings something to life, there is silence. Even God paused between commands, a breath between each *"Let there be."*

When you enter silence, you return to the field before form, the womb of divine potential.

It is here that the blueprint becomes clear again. It is here that your vibration resets.

"Be still, and know that I am God.", Psalm 46:10

Stillness is sacred architecture. It builds strength without effort. It allows Heaven to speak the next line of your unfolding creation.

The Architecture of Love

At the highest level, all creation is built from one material: Love.

Every star, every breath, every thought is formed of its resonance. When your thoughts align with love, they harmonize with the Creator's blueprint. When they drift into fear, they build false structures that cannot last.

Love endures because love is truth. When you create from love, you build eternity into your design.

"Whoever lives in love lives in God, and God in them.", 1 John 4:16

Your destiny, therefore, is not to construct a life that impresses the world, but to build a vibration that welcomes Heaven.

Prayer of the Silent Architect

Beloved Creator, teach me the art of holy construction.

May my thoughts be true, my intentions be clear, and my actions be filled with love.

Where I have built from fear, dismantle the walls with grace.

Where I have doubted, strengthen my faith.

Let the temple of my life be designed by Your wisdom and built upon the foundation of peace.

Amen.

Reflection

Every soul is an architect of vibration, each thought a beam of light, each emotion a pillar of energy, each action a brick of faith.

You are constructing your reality not through effort, but through resonance.

When your mind aligns with Heaven, your life aligns with harmony. When your heart rests in love, your world reflects that same design.

Nothing you build in love can ever be lost. It is eternal architecture, the invisible cathedral of grace that stretches from your soul to the stars.

THE LIVING CATHEDRAL, HOW THE BODY, MIND, AND SPIRIT BECOME THE HOUSE OF LIGHT

Your body is not a shell; it is a sanctuary. It was never meant to be at war with your spirit, but to be its vessel of revelation, a living cathedral where divine energy gathers, resonates, and expresses love through motion, sensation, and breath.

"Do you not know that you are God's temple and that God's Spirit dwells in you?", 1 Corinthians 3:16

Every cell is an altar. Every breath is incense rising. Every heartbeat is a prayer drum echoing through eternity. Your body was crafted not merely to survive, but to sing, to vibrate in harmony with Heaven's rhythm.

When you live with awareness, you realize that God does not dwell above you; He dwells through you. You are the cathedral, and the light of Christ is the flame that burns within.

The Architecture of the Body

Just as a cathedral has arches, pillars, and chambers designed to carry sound and light, your body is also a sacred structure.

Your spine is the pillar of divine alignment, your heart the rose window that filters light into color and emotion, your breath the wind through the corridors of prayer.

When your body is in balance, spirit moves easily through you, a living flow of grace.

When it is clouded by tension, resentment, or neglect, the resonance falters, and the music of divine awareness becomes muffled.

This is not punishment. It is an invitation, a reminder to return to the sacredness of embodiment.

Your body is not a hindrance to holiness. It is the vessel through which holiness experiences itself.

The Nervous System: God's Instrument of Light

The nervous system is the temple's wiring, the network that translates divine signals into perception and response.

When you meditate, pray, or breathe deeply, you regulate this divine circuitry. You move from chaos to coherence, from reaction to response, from fear to peace.

Science now shows that states of gratitude and love produce synchronized heart and brain waves, a measurable pattern of harmony.

This is not a coincidence. It is evidence that the body was designed to mirror Heaven's order.

When you breathe with awareness, you calm the electric storm of anxiety and restore your internal rhythm to grace.

This is how prayer heals. It is not magic, it is resonance.

The Body as a Choir of Cells

Every organ, every cell, every strand of DNA sings a note in the symphony of your being.

Your heart keeps rhythm, your lungs add melody, your skin vibrates with the harmonics of the world around you.

When one part falls out of tune, the entire symphony feels dissonant, but healing comes when you listen, when you treat your body not as an object to fix, but as a choir member to guide gently back into harmony.

Food, movement, rest, and thought are your instruments of tuning.

When you eat whole, living foods, you feed light to light. When you walk in nature, you step into the cathedral's vast sanctuary of sound. When you rest, you allow the choir to retune itself to God's frequency.

"In Him we live and move and have our being.", Acts 17:28

You are never separate from the divine energy that sustains you; you are its living expression.

Mind as the Choir Director

The mind facilitates the flow between the spirit and the body. It chooses which vibration dominates: fear or faith, complaint or gratitude.

When the mind quiets, the heart takes lead, and divine rhythm restores itself.

But when the mind resists, when it obsesses, doubts, or condemns, it interrupts the harmony.

That is why stillness and prayer are not luxuries but necessities. They clear the static so the spirit can move freely again.

"Let this mind be in you which was also in Christ Jesus.", Philippians 2:5

To hold the mind of Christ is to think from the frequency of love, to interpret every experience as an opportunity for compassion.

When you do this, the temple lights up from within, neurons firing in patterns of peace, cells radiating joy.

Spirit as the Choir's Song

Spirit is the living melody that animates all. It moves through you, through everyone, through everything.

You cannot lose it. You can only forget to hear it.

The Spirit's song rises in you through intuition, laughter, tears, the moments that remind you you're alive.

When you feel awe at sunrise, at kindness, at forgiveness, you are hearing Spirit sing.

When you love without condition, you become the song itself.

Vibrational Maintenance of the Temple

Just as ancient cathedrals require care to preserve their beauty, so does your body temple require loving attention.

Care for it not from vanity, but reverence. Drink water as baptism, eat with gratitude, rest as worship.

Be mindful of what enters your senses: words, images, and emotions. Everything you absorb becomes part of the temple's resonance.

Choose peace as your architecture. Choose forgiveness as your light. Choose laughter as your restoration.

Grace maintains the temple; awareness opens its doors.

Healing Through Harmony

True healing is not the removal of pain, but the restoration of vibration.

When the heart forgives, cells respond. When the mind releases judgment, the body exhales.

Every act of love recalibrates the temple. Every act of compassion rings like a bell in its halls.

You are not healing alone; you are resonating with Heaven's infinite pattern of wholeness.

This is why miracles happen quietly, not as interruptions of nature, but as the natural consequence of returning to divine order.

Prayer of the Living Cathedral

Beloved Creator, architect of body and soul, let me honor the temple You have made of me.

Teach me to listen to its music, to feed it light, to rest it in grace.

Let my mind be clear, my heart be open, my spirit be free.

May every thought, every step, every breath resound with Your glory.

I am your sanctuary.

Amen.

Reflection

Your body is the chapel of the Eternal. Your mind is the altar of awareness. Your spirit is the flame that burns within them both.

You do not need to reach for Heaven; you are already standing in its sanctuary.

When you breathe with gratitude, you light the candles. When you love, you open the stained-glass windows. When you forgive, you let sunlight stream in.

You are not merely living, you are worshipping through every heartbeat, every breath, every thought of love.

The cathedral of you stands eternal, and within it, the Christ light never fades.

THE LIGHT WITHIN THE SHADOW, HOW PAIN AND DARKNESS BECOME PATHWAYS TO DIVINE ILLUMINATION

In every soul's journey, there comes a time when the light dims. Prayers seem to echo into emptiness, and what once felt radiant becomes heavy and unclear. The world appears silent, and your heart, even though it beats, feels hollow.

This is not abandonment. It is an initiation. The shadow is not the absence of God; it is the space where His light prepares to reveal its most actual strength.

"Even the darkness will not be dark to You; the night will shine like the day, for darkness is as light to You.", Psalm 139:12

When you stand within your shadow, grief, loss, fear, guilt, exhaustion, you are not being punished. You are being purified. The light that once surrounded you now moves within you, searching for places still unlit, still unloved, still hidden.

The shadow is where love goes to find you.

The Purpose of Darkness

Darkness is not the opposite of light; it is its womb.

Just as a seed must rest in soil before it grows, the soul must sometimes rest in shadow before it can bloom into understanding.

The ancients understood this: night is not the death of day, it is its completion. The stars are not distant; they are reminders that even in the deepest dark, light multiplies quietly.

So when your life feels shrouded in confusion or sorrow, remember: you are in sacred ground. Something unseen is germinating. The soul grows roots before it grows wings.

The Emotional Alchemy of Pain

Pain is energy condensed, a vibration slowed to the point of density. When held in awareness, it transforms. When resisted, it stagnates.

Every tear is frequently releasing. Every sigh is energy transmuting.

Science tells us emotion is energy in motion. Spirit tells us emotion is prayer in disguise.

Pain, then, is the teacher of transformation. It asks you to feel so deeply that nothing false can remain. It carves space where grace may enter.

When you let yourself feel, without judgment, without rushing, you turn suffering into sacred fire. And that fire refines the soul until only love remains.

"Blessed are those who mourn, for they shall be comforted.", Matthew 5:4

To mourn is to open the temple gates of the heart, allowing comfort, divine vibration, to flow in.

The Vibrational Shadow

Every being emits light, and where there is light, there will be shadow. But shadow is not evil; it is information.

It reveals what remains unhealed, what remains unloved.

Your anger reveals boundaries that need respect. Your fear points to faith waiting to awaken. Your sorrow shows where love still wants to flow.

To reject your shadow is to deny the very soil from which your light grows. To embrace it with compassion is to turn darkness into revelation.

"The light shines in the darkness, and the darkness has not overcome it.", John 1:5

The light does not destroy the dark; it transforms it. That is how grace works, not by denial, but by illumination.

The Shadow of the Christ

Even Jesus walked through the valley of the shadow. He wept, He questioned, He bled. On the cross, His cry, *"My God, my God, why have You forsaken me?"*, was not despair but revelation: the human experience of separation made sacred.

Through His darkness, He bridged the chasm between God and humankind.

So too, when you walk through your pain, you walk in His footsteps. Each tear aligns you closer with His compassion, each moment of surrender draws Heaven closer to Earth.

The crucifixion is not only history; it is energy, the vibration of transformation that passes through every soul on its journey back to love.

When the Light Withdraws

Sometimes, God hides not to punish, but to teach you to see Him everywhere.

When the light withdraws, it invites you to become the light yourself.

You learn that peace cannot depend on circumstance, that love must rise from within even when the world falls silent.

The mystics called this the night of the soul, not because it is cruel, but because it strips away illusion.

When you have lost everything that isn't love, what remains is love itself.

The Quantum Heart of Healing

At the smallest level of existence, light behaves both as a particle and a wave. It collapses into form only when observed, meaning consciousness determines creation.

Similarly, spiritual healing occurs when awareness meets pain.

When you look at your suffering with compassion, you change its structure. The wave of despair gives way to understanding. The particle of grief becomes gratitude.

You literally rewire the vibration of the memory. This is the alchemy of divine awareness, science meeting spirit in the heart's laboratory.

"The eye is the lamp of the body. If your eye is healthy, your whole body will be full of light. ", Matthew 6:22

To look upon your pain with faith is to let light enter every cell of your being.

Embracing the Shadow with Love

The shadow is never asking for punishment. It is asking to be seen.

When you turn toward your sorrow and whisper, *"I love you still,"* something ancient is released.

You reclaim the part of yourself that believed it was unworthy of light. You welcome home the prodigal fragments of your soul.

Every time you do this, you become more whole. You become the Christ-light remembering itself through matter.

Forgive yourself for not feeling holy all the time. Forgive your anger, your confusion, your exhaustion. They, too, are prayers, raw, unpolished, but heard in Heaven's deepest chambers.

The Transformational Equation

Darkness + Awareness = Light.

That is the formula of redemption.

Wherever you bring awareness, the divine gaze dissolves darkness. You do not have to fight it. You simply have to illuminate it.

The moment you say, *"Here I am,"* the shadow begins to shift. Light does not need to overpower darkness; it only needs to enter it.

And once light enters, darkness ceases to be darkness at all.

The Resurrection Within

Every crucifixion of the soul contains the seed of resurrection. When your heart breaks, something eternal begins to bloom through the cracks.

The resurrection is not an event in history; it is the eternal truth of transformation. Every time you forgive, you rise. Every time you choose hope, you roll away the stone. Every time you love again after loss, you walk out of the tomb.

You are the living continuation of that divine pattern.

"I am the resurrection and the life.", John 11:25

Christ was not declaring exclusivity; He was revealing identity. He is the light in you that cannot die.

Prayer of the Shadow and the Light

Beloved Christ, when my heart feels heavy and my sight dim, remind me that You dwell within both the shadow and the flame.

Let me not fear my darkness, but enter it with courage and compassion.

Transform my pain into prayer, my fear into faith, my sorrow into song.

May every shadow become a doorway to You. Amen.

Reflection

You are not meant to erase the shadow; you are meant to love it into light.

The darkness that once frightened you will one day be your teacher, the womb from which your new awareness is born.

When you stand at the edge of your sorrow, know this: you are not alone. The same Christ who wept also rose, and He walks beside you through every valley.

The shadow is not your enemy; it is your initiation. And when you emerge from it, your light will no longer be fragile or borrowed. It will be yours, steady, radiant, and eternal.

THE FREQUENCY OF FORGIVENESS, HEALING THE HEART'S MAGNETIC FIELD

There are energies so powerful they can heal what words cannot touch. Forgiveness is one of them.

It is not a thought, not a decision of the mind alone, but a vibration of the heart, a tuning of the soul back to love's original frequency.

"And when ye stand praying, forgive, if ye have ought against any: that your Father also which is in heaven may forgive you your trespasses. ", Mark 11:25

Forgiveness is not about permission. It is about liberation, the freedom to breathe again without the gravity of resentment pulling your energy down.

When you forgive, you do not excuse what happened. You simply stop carrying it as your own wound. You let the light take the weight.

You are not letting someone else off the hook; you are letting yourself off the cross.

The Science of the Heart

The human heart is not just a muscle; it is an electromagnetic instrument of divine intelligence.

The HeartMath Institute discovered that the heart's electromagnetic field is sixty times stronger than that of the brain. It extends several feet beyond the body, constantly sending and receiving frequencies of emotion and thought.

When you hold anger, grief, or fear, the field becomes incoherent, like static interrupting a broadcast. Your energy weakens, your immunity drops, and clarity fades.

But when you forgive, the field restores coherence. The rhythm of the heart synchronizes with the breath, and your entire system hums in harmony with the divine field of love.

Forgiveness is not just spiritual healing; it is a form of vibrational medicine.

The Physics of Release

Unforgiveness is a form of energetic entanglement. It binds two souls in a feedback loop of pain. The moment you hold resentment, your energy becomes connected to the person or event in question, a tether through which an emotional current continues to flow.

You replay the story, and every retelling strengthens the cord.

But forgiveness severs that loop, not by cutting it with vengeance, but by dissolving it in compassion.

In physics, when two particles become entangled, a change in one instantly affects the other, no matter how far apart they are. Forgiveness works the same way. The moment you release someone energetically, the vibration shifts in both hearts.

You cannot control what they do with that release, but you are free. And your freedom alters the world's field.

Forgiveness as Frequency Correction

Think of forgiveness as spiritual tuning. When your heart vibrates in bitterness, it plays out of tune with divine love. Every interaction echoes that dissonance.

But when you forgive, your heart re-tunes to love's frequency, the Christ frequency, and your entire life begins to resonate with harmony again.

You begin to attract gentler experiences, more authentic people, and circumstances that align with your peace rather than your pain.

"Create in me a clean heart, O God; and renew a right spirit within me.", Psalm 51:10

Forgiveness is how the heart cleans itself. It is spiritual hygiene, a daily washing of the soul in light.

The Emotional Mechanics of Forgiveness

Forgiveness often begins as resistance. The mind says, *"I can't forgive that."* And that's all right. Forgiveness is not an act of pretending. It begins in honesty.

You must feel the pain before you can release it. If you skip that step, the energy only hides deeper.

The process moves like this:

1. **Recognition:** I was hurt.
2. **Acknowledgment:** The pain is real.
3. **Acceptance:** It happened, and I cannot change it.
4. **Release:** I choose not to let it define me.
5. **Reconnection:** I align with love again.

At the moment of release, your energy field recalibrates. Your heartbeat steadies. The temple within you fills with light.

Forgiveness is the nervous system's return to divine rhythm.

Forgiving the Self

The most difficult forgiveness is often the one directed inward.

We replay our choices, our words, our failures, as though punishing ourselves could somehow rewrite them.

But guilt, when held too long, becomes spiritual corrosion. It blocks the flow of love, not because God withholds it, but because shame refuses to receive it.

To forgive yourself is to agree with Heaven that you are still worthy of light.

"There is therefore now no condemnation for those who are in Christ Jesus.", Romans 8:1

God does not remember what you keep reliving. He remembers only your essence, the spark of Himself that never falters.

When you forgive yourself, you reopen the gate for divine current to move freely again.

Forgiving When It Feels Impossible

Some wounds run deep: betrayal, abuse, and abandonment. The human mind may never justify them, and that's because forgiveness is not of the mind.

You cannot reason yourself into peace. You must vibrate into it.

Sometimes the prayer is not *"I forgive,"* but *"Lord, make me willing to forgive."*

Willingness begins the vibrational shift. Grace does the rest.

When you whisper that prayer, Christ moves through your resistance like light through a stained-glass window, turning pain into beauty, brokenness into color.

Forgiveness, then, becomes less about effort and more about surrender.

You don't do forgiveness. You allow it to happen through you.

The Alchemy of Forgiveness

Forgiveness transforms energy. It changes what was toxic into nourishment.

When you forgive, you reclaim the energy you once spent on remembering the pain. That reclaimed energy becomes wisdom, empathy, and creativity. It becomes light.

Every saint, every mystic, every healed soul has walked through this same fire, the fire that burns away bitterness and leaves only compassion.

"Father, forgive them, for they know not what they do.", Luke 23:34

In that single sentence, Jesus redefined power. He showed us that the highest vibration is not dominance but mercy.

Forgiveness does not make you weak. It makes you like Him.

Healing the Heart's Magnetic Field

When you forgive, your heart emits a higher electromagnetic frequency. It communicates peace to the nervous system, signals the immune system to repair, and expands your field to touch others with invisible grace.

The energy of love radiates beyond your body, calming those near you, harmonizing discordant spaces, and shifting the collective vibration of humanity itself.

Forgiveness is how you heal the world, one vibration at a time.

You become a living transmitter of divine coherence, a heartbeat that whispers to others, It's safe to return to love.

Prayer of Forgiveness

Beloved Light of Christ, soften my heart where it has hardened, and open my breath where it has closed.

Teach me to forgive not with my mind, but with the frequency of my soul.

Where anger lingers, let compassion rise. Where pain echoes, let peace sing.

Free me from the cords of resentment and let my heart be the tuning fork of love once more.

I release all that binds me to sorrow. I choose the rhythm of forgiveness. I return to You. Amen.

Reflection

Forgiveness is not the end of pain; it is the transformation of it.

When you forgive, you realign with the heartbeat of Christ, the rhythm that holds the universe together.

You become part of the music of redemption, a note that never fades.

And from that note, others begin to resonate. The more you forgive, the more light flows through you, until one day, you realize you are no longer carrying the wound at all.

You are carrying the song.

THE RESONANCE OF GRATITUDE, HOW THANKFULNESS EXPANDS THE SOUL'S LIGHT

Gratitude is the sound of the soul returning home. It is the frequency of remembrance, the vibration that realigns the heart to the rhythm of Heaven.

When you say *"thank You,"* you open a portal through which light rushes in. Gratitude turns pain into wisdom, loss into blessing, and ordinary breath into prayer.

"Give thanks in all circumstances; for this is God's will for you in Christ Jesus.", 1 Thessalonians 5:18

This is not a command to ignore suffering, but an invitation to transcend it. Gratitude does not deny what is hard; it expands your perception until you can see the light that has always been shining within it.

The Physics of Gratitude

Every emotion has a measurable frequency. Fear vibrates at a low and constricted frequency, while gratitude radiates at one of the highest quantifiable frequencies of human experience.

Scientific studies have shown that consistent gratitude can lower blood pressure, stabilize heart rhythms, and enhance immune response.

But beyond biology, gratitude reorganizes energy itself. It shifts the electromagnetic field of the heart, creating coherence between body, mind, and spirit.

When you are grateful, your brain releases dopamine and serotonin, the same chemicals associated with joy and peace. Your nervous system relaxes, your breath deepens, and the world around you begins to respond differently.

Gratitude, quite literally, changes the field.

The Spiritual Law of Amplification

What you appreciate, appreciates. This is both metaphysical truth and divine law.

When you express gratitude, you align your consciousness with abundance, and abundance responds.

Every thought is a signal, and gratitude is the signal of *"more light, please."*

"For to everyone who has, more will be given, and he will have abundance.", Matthew 25:29

This verse is not about possession; it is about vibration. When you recognize a blessing, you multiply its energy. When you dwell in lack, you shrink your capacity to receive.

The universe, like a mirror, reflects your internal tone. When your heart hums in gratitude, creation hums with you.

The Hidden Power of Simple Thanks

Gratitude is not reserved for great miracles. It is the quiet acknowledgment of the small, the warmth of sunlight on your skin, the rhythm of your breath, the presence of someone who stayed when they didn't have to.

When you give thanks for what is simple, you open space for the miraculous.

Every *"thank You"* sends out a wave of coherence that ripples through creation. It blesses not only your life but the lives of all who share your energetic field.

Heaven measures not the grandeur of your gratitude, but its sincerity.

The whispered *"thank You"* in the dark carries as much power as the songs of angels.

Gratitude and the Brain of Light

Neuroscience shows that the more often we practice gratitude, the more the brain's neural pathways rewire themselves toward positivity.

What begins as practice becomes habit. What starts as a habit becomes an integral part of one's identity. And identity shapes reality.

When you train the mind to see blessing first, you literally alter your perception of the world.

Light is not added; it is revealed.

"The eye is the lamp of the body. If your eyes are healthy, your whole body will be full of light. ", Matthew 6:22

To see through the lens of gratitude is to restore clarity to the inner eye, the soul's perception of divine presence in all things.

The Vibrational Signature of Thanksgiving

Imagine your heart as a radiant sphere of light. Each thought, emotion, and word sends ripples outward, waves of energy that inform the world around you.

When you speak in gratitude, those ripples shine with harmony. They attract peace, favor, and grace back to you because you are resonating with the creative frequency of God.

Gratitude is the vibration of alignment, the state where your heart's magnet aligns with the divine current of abundance.

This is why miracles follow thankful hearts. Gratitude doesn't earn blessings; it reveals your readiness to receive them.

When Gratitude Feels Far Away

There are moments when gratitude feels impossible, when grief numbs your voice, and thankfulness seems like betrayal of your pain.

In those moments, God does not ask you to be cheerful. He asks only that you be willing to see His light again.

Even a sigh of willingness, *"Lord, I want to be grateful again"*, changes your vibration.

Gratitude begins not with having, but with seeing.

And sometimes the smallest act of recognition, a sunrise, a child's laughter, the quiet mercy of being able to breathe, becomes the key that unlocks the door.

The Communion of Gratitude

When Jesus broke bread, He gave thanks.

That moment, so simple and so divine, was not a ritual of manners. It was an act of vibrational alignment. He lifted the ordinary into the eternal.

"And He took bread, gave thanks and broke it, and gave it to them, saying, 'This is My body given for you; do this in remembrance of Me.'", Luke 22:19

In giving thanks, He infused matter with meaning. He showed us that gratitude transforms the physical world into a vessel of divine love.

Every time you give thanks, you perform the same miracle. You turn life into a sacrament. You make the mundane holy.

Gratitude as the Language of Heaven

The angels do not speak in words but in vibration. Their language is gratitude, a constant praise that sustains the universe.

When you practice gratitude, you join that celestial song. Your heart becomes an instrument in the symphony of creation.

Every *"thank You"* is music, every breath of appreciation a note of light that echoes through eternity.

"Enter His gates with thanksgiving and His courts with praise.", Psalm 100:4

Gratitude is the key that unlocks the gates of Heaven, not someday, but here and now.

When you give thanks, Heaven enters you.

The Vibrational Field of Gratitude

Your gratitude changes environments. It cleanses rooms, softens arguments, and invites healing where there was tension.

People feel it, even when you say nothing.

Gratitude radiates silently through the electromagnetic field like warmth through sunlight. It alters not just your mind, but the minds of those around you.

When you are thankful, you broadcast stability, peace, and love, signals the world desperately needs.

Gratitude is activism of the soul. It heals without words.

Prayer of Gratitude

Beloved Source of Light, You fill my lungs with breath, my heart with rhythm, my life with the beauty of being.

Let me see You in all things. Let my first word each morning and my last each night be *"Thank You."*

Teach me to give thanks in shadow and in light, in sorrow and in song.

May my gratitude ripple outward to heal what I cannot see and bless what I cannot reach.

For You, O Lord, are the Giver and the Gift, and my soul remembers You in praise. Amen.

Reflection

Gratitude is the breath of grace. It is the evidence that love is alive within you.

Each time you give thanks, you expand the field of light around you. You remind creation that goodness is still here. You remind yourself that God never left.

The soul that lives in gratitude becomes a light to others, a walking sunrise, a silent prayer of peace.

And when you reach that vibration, you will understand: Heaven is not a destination. It is the frequency of a grateful heart.

THE BREATH OF ETERNITY: AWAKENING TO THE DIVINE PULSE OF CREATION

In the beginning, there was breath. Before sound, before word, before form, the universe inhaled.

That breath became wind, wave, motion, and life. It carried the vibration of love across endless darkness and whispered existence into being.

Every exhale since that first breath is the echo of God's heartbeat expanding through eternity.

"Then the Lord God formed man of the dust of the ground, and breathed into his nostrils the breath of life; and man became a living soul. ", Genesis 2:7

That sacred moment was not history; it is happening now. Every inhale is Genesis renewed, and every exhale is creation continuing through you.

You are not separate from the Divine breath. You are the Divine breath given form, given voice, given memory.

The Breath as the Bridge Between Worlds

Breath is the invisible thread that connects the finite to the infinite. It is the bridge between body and spirit, between matter and motion, between silence and song.

When you breathe, you exchange energy with the universe. You take in what the trees release, you release what the stars once breathed. The breath you draw now has circled the world through countless lives, carrying prayers, laughter, and whispered hopes.

Inhaling, you receive. Exhaling, you give. You are part of an eternal circulation, a rhythm of divine reciprocity.

And in that rhythm, you remember who you are.

"The Spirit of God has made me, and the breath of the Almighty gives me life.", Job 33:4

The same Spirit that breathed galaxies into motion breathes through your lungs this very moment.

The Physics of Sacred Air

Air is matter in motion, unseen but real, invisible yet capable of shaping mountains, waves, and destiny. In vibration, breath becomes sound; in sound, it becomes word; in word, it becomes creation.

Even science now tells us that breath alters brain waves, heart rhythm, and emotion. Slow, conscious breathing synchronizes the brain's hemispheres, balances the nervous system, and creates electromagnetic coherence in the heart.

This is why prayer calms, why meditation heals, why sighs release tension the way rain clears the air.

Your breath is the body's direct link to divine intelligence.

When you breathe with awareness, you activate the inner temple, the Living Cathedral of God's energy within you.

Breathing in the Name of Love

In Hebrew, the word ruach, which means breath, also refers to spirit, wind, or divine movement. In Sanskrit, it is prana. In Greek, pneuma. Each culture knew: the invisible air that sustains us is the presence of the Creator moving through creation.

When Jesus breathed on His disciples and said, *"Receive the Holy Spirit"* (John 20:22), He wasn't performing a symbol; He was transmitting vibration. His breath carried divine frequency, the remembrance of Oneness.

To breathe consciously is to receive that same Spirit again.

Every inhale says, *"You are alive."* Every exhale whispers, *"You are loved."* Together they form the heartbeat of Heaven: I am… I am… I am.

The Quantum Field of Breath

Every breath creates a ripple in the quantum field. The electromagnetic pulse from your heart and lungs extends outward, touching the world around you.

When your breathing is shallow or anxious, your field contracts, and your world feels smaller. When your breathing deepens in peace, your field expands, and life responds in kind.

This is why prayerful breath can alter not only the self but the space around you.

The calm person in the room helps calm the rest of the room. The centered heart anchors others in a state of invisible peace. This is not mysticism; it is resonance.

To breathe in love is to breathe in God's frequency. To breathe out compassion is to become His echo in the world.

Breath as Memory of Eternity

Each breath carries the memory of the stars. Hydrogen, the element of water and life, was forged in the birth of galaxies. The atoms in your lungs were once fire in distant suns.

You are literally breathing the cosmos. The dust of stars, the wind of ancient forests, the prayers of those who came before, they live within your every inhale.

And through you, God continues His eternal exhalation.

"Let everything that has breath praise the Lord.", Psalm 150:6

Breath itself is praise. Every exhale says, *"I surrender."* Every inhale says, *"I receive."*

To breathe consciously is to pray without ceasing.

The Breath and the Christ Within

The Christ-light within you breathes eternally. It is the pulse behind your pulse, the rhythm behind your breath.

When you slow down and listen, you will feel it, a steady, luminous hum at the center of your being. That is the Holy Spirit, breathing you as much as you breathe It.

Even in grief, the Spirit breathes for you. Even in silence, it keeps time. Even when you feel faith has left, it is the breath that prays on your behalf.

"The Spirit Himself intercedes for us with groanings too deep for words.", Romans 8:26

The breath is that intercession, God moving through the human form, sustaining you when you cannot sustain yourself.

When you exhale your pain into the presence of Christ, He transforms it into peace. When you inhale again, you draw that peace back as strength.

Breath as Light in Motion

In stillness, you can see it, the light that moves with the rhythm of breath.

Every inhale gathers the golden radiance of the divine; every exhale sends it through your body, healing, balancing, renewing.

In moments of despair, breathe light through the heart. See it circulate through your body like a river of grace washing every cell clean.

Breathe until you remember that love and oxygen are made of the same essence; they both give life freely.

The act of breathing is God's daily miracle inside you.

The Breath of the World

When you breathe in peace, the world breathes easier. When you breathe in anger, the world holds its breath.

Your inhale and exhale are part of the collective respiration of humanity. Each breath contributes to the atmosphere, both energetically and physically.

This is why stillness matters. Your peace becomes oxygen for the soul of the planet. Your awareness feeds the universal field.

When many breathe consciously together, storms quiet, violence pauses, and love expands.

You are not just breathing in God, you are breathing with God. You are His rhythm in human form.

A Prayer of Eternal Breath

Divine Breath of Life, move through me as You moved through the first dawn.

Fill my lungs with Your presence, and let me exhale Your peace.

Teach me to breathe not only air, but love.

Let my breath be prayer, my exhale be surrender, my inhale be remembrance.

May every breath I take remind me that You are nearer than my pulse, deeper than my thoughts, and forever within me.

Breathe me, O Lord, until the world remembers the sound of Heaven again. Amen.

Reflection

You are the breath of eternity clothed in form. You are the exhale of a loving God and the inhale of creation returning home.

Every breath you take is a vow, a promise that love continues, that life renews, that light is unbroken.

When you breathe with awareness, you no longer pray for God to come close; you awaken to the truth that He never left.

His breath is your life, and your life is His whisper in time.

THE MIRROR OF COMPASSION: SEEING CHRIST IN EVERY FACE

There is a moment in the soul's journey when you stop asking where God is and begin to see Him everywhere.

In the eyes of the weary. In the laughter of a child. In the stranger who pauses to hold a door. In the one who hurt you, for even there, beneath the wound, the divine spark waits to be seen again.

"Truly I tell you, whatever you did for one of the least of these brothers and sisters of Mine, you did for Me.", Matthew 25:40

Compassion is not pity. It is recognition, the moment when the veil between you and another dissolves and you remember that there was never separation at all.

When you look through the eyes of love, you see not the mask of humanity, but the face of Christ looking back at you.

The Mirror of Awareness

The outer world mirrors the inner. Every encounter reflects the vibration you carry.

When you are full of judgment, you see division. When you are full of love, you see connection.

This is not punishment; it is perception. The universe, like a compassionate teacher, shows you what you believe, so that you may choose again.

When you meet anger with peace, you break the mirror of conflict and reveal the light beneath the surface.

Compassion, then, is not merely feeling for someone; it is feeling with them, a resonance of heart frequencies aligning in grace.

Science confirms this divine resonance: the human heart emits measurable electromagnetic waves that can synchronize with the heart rhythms of others. When you stand in love, you literally help another's heart remember its own peace.

You become a living blessing.

The Eyes of the Christ Within

To see Christ in another requires first recognizing Him within yourself.

If you believe yourself unworthy, you will not believe another capable of holiness. If you only see flaws in yourself, you will likely search for flaws in others.

But when you see the divine breath animating your own being, you cannot help but see it shining in all creation.

"The light shines in the darkness, and the darkness has not overcome it.", John 1:5

That same light is in the eyes of everyone you meet. It may be hidden under fear, shame, or pain, but it is there, unextinguished, unaltered, eternal.

When you choose to see through the lens of compassion, you become a participant in God's vision, you know what He sees: the unbroken soul beneath every story.

The Vibrational Field of Compassion

Compassion is energy in motion, the frequency of divine empathy. It is love translated into vibration.

When you feel compassion, your heart releases oxytocin, the *"bonding hormone"* that creates trust and safety. Your nervous system relaxes; your body emits coherent waves of peace. Those waves ripple outward, touching others whether or not words are spoken.

In that moment, you become an instrument of healing.

Every act of kindness, a gentle word, a patient pause, a hand extended instead of withheld, sends measurable frequencies of harmony into the world.

Heaven rejoices in such acts because through them, Christ continues His ministry of love on Earth.

The Compassionate Frequency

Compassion vibrates higher than sympathy. Sympathy says, *"I feel sorry for you."* Compassion says, *"I see you, I love you, I walk with you."*

One observes from above; the other kneels beside.

When Jesus healed, He never healed from pity. He healed from compassion, from identification with wholeness.

He looked upon the blind and saw vision. He looked upon the sinner and saw purity. He looked upon death and saw resurrection.

His gaze did not reflect condition; it revealed truth.

"When He saw the crowds, He was moved with compassion for them, because they were harassed and helpless, like sheep without a shepherd.", Matthew 9:36

Moved, that is the key. Compassion does not remain still; it becomes action.

The divine vibration within you cannot remain dormant once recognized; it seeks to express itself as mercy, service, or grace.

The Psychology of Compassion

From a psychological view, compassion softens the brain's defense mechanisms. It lowers amygdala activity, the part responsible for fear and anger, and strengthens the prefrontal cortex, the region tied to empathy, reason, and moral awareness.

In simple terms, the more compassion you practice, the more capable you become of love.

Compassion literally changes your perception. You stop seeing enemies and start seeing teachers. You stop defending and start understanding. And in understanding, you heal the illusion of separation.

Loving the Difficult Faces

It is easy to see Christ in the gentle and kind. The challenge is to see Him in those who wound.

But remember: darkness hides pain, not evil. The unkind heart is wounded, the cruel word a cry for help misdirected.

Compassion does not mean staying in harm's way; it means seeing the soul behind the shadow and praying for its awakening, even as you protect your peace.

"Love your enemies, bless those who curse you, do good to those who hate you, and pray for those who mistreat you. ", Matthew 5:44

This teaching is not about weakness. It is about vibration. To bless instead of curse is to maintain your frequency of grace. You do not absorb their darkness; you amplify your light.

And light always wins.

The Compassion of Self

You cannot pour from an empty vessel. Genuine compassion must begin within.

The heart that cannot forgive itself struggles to forgive others. The soul that neglects its own rest cannot give peace freely.

Self-compassion is not selfishness. It aligns with divine mercy. It is saying to yourself, *"I, too, am a child of God. I, too, am learning to love."*

When you offer yourself kindness, your vibration lifts. Your capacity to love multiplies. And the mirror of your being reflects grace more clearly into the world.

The World as Reflection

As you awaken compassion within yourself, the world begins to mirror it back.

Situations once filled with tension now soften. Relationships once heavy begin to heal. Even strangers seem lighter, as though the universe itself responds to your gentler gaze.

You realize the truth: it was never the world that needed changing, it was the way you saw it.

When perception shifts, reality rearranges. And everywhere you look, you begin to see Christ smiling back.

Prayer of Compassion

Beloved Christ, open the eyes of my heart that I may see You in every face.

Teach me to look beyond words and wounds to the soul that longs to be remembered.

Let my kindness be Your hands, my words Your healing voice, my heart Your open door.

When I forget and fall into judgment, remind me that there is no *"other"*, only You, wearing a thousand faces.

May I live as Your reflection, a mirror of mercy, a vessel of compassion. Amen.

Reflection

Compassion is the highest seeing, not through the eyes, but through the heart.

It turns every encounter into communion, every moment into ministry.

To live with compassion is to live as Christ did, to walk the world as a mirror of love until all who look upon you remember what they truly are.

When you see Him in others, you awaken Him within yourself. And one by one, through the quiet power of your gaze, the world begins to shine again.

THE CIRCLE OF GRACE: LIVING THE LIGHT IN DAILY LIFE

There comes a time in every soul's awakening when the question shifts from *"Where is God?"* to *"How may I live as God's love?"*

This is the true flowering of faith, when belief turns to embodiment, when prayer becomes movement, and the light within you begins to illuminate the path before you.

The circle of grace is not a doctrine; it is a living rhythm, a continual flow of giving and receiving, of breathing in the divine and breathing it out into the world.

"Freely you have received; freely give.", Matthew 10:8

Grace does not end when it enters you; it completes itself when it passes through you. You are not the destination of light, but its continuation.

And as you live it, you become a living testament of Heaven on Earth.

The Motion of Grace

Grace is movement, never static, never stagnant. It flows like water, filling every low place with healing, finding every crevice where love has not yet reached.

When you hold peace within yourself, you send it out like ripples from a stone cast into still water. It travels through your words, your gestures, even your thoughts.

The world is touched by what moves through you.

You may never know how far one smile travels, how deeply one act of forgiveness echoes, or how a single prayer of compassion can shift unseen tides in another soul's life.

Grace is infinite; its effects multiply beyond time.

Everyday Acts of Light

You do not need to perform great miracles to change the world. You need only live as a vessel of kindness, letting love guide even the smallest choices.

Hold the door open. Speak gently. Feed someone's hunger, not only of body, but of heart. Listen without judgment. Say thank you. Say I love you. Say nothing when silence would heal more than words.

The light that shines through such acts is not ordinary. It is eternal.

"Let your light so shine before men, that they may see your good works and glorify your Father in Heaven.", Matthew 5:16

To live as light is to live in continuous worship, not confined to temples, but carried through every breath, every touch, every thought aligned with love.

Grace as Reciprocity

The circle of grace is a continual exchange, divine energy flowing between Heaven and Earth, giver and receiver, you and all creation.

When you give from love, you are not depleted; you are renewed. When you receive with gratitude, you expand the flow even more.

Grace cannot be hoarded; it thrives in circulation.

Think of the body, the heart pumps blood not to keep it, but to sustain life throughout the whole. So it is with grace. To stop giving is to stop the flow.

When you share love, you complete the divine circuit.

Grace at Work, in Home, and in the World

To live gracefully is to bring divine awareness into every environment you enter.

At work, grace may mean patience with chaos, seeing co-workers not as competitors but collaborators in purpose. At home, it may mean gentleness in tone, forgiveness after conflict, the courage to listen without defending.

In public, grace may appear as respect, kindness to strangers, and care for the Earth that sustains you.

Each act, no matter how small, sends light into places it is rarely seen.

Even when no one witnesses it, Heaven does. And the vibration of that act joins the great symphony of divine renewal.

When You Forget the Flow

There will be moments when the current feels lost, when exhaustion, anger, or fear clouds your peace. But even that is part of the circle.

Grace is not broken by forgetfulness; it simply waits for you to remember.

When you fall out of alignment, pause. Breathe. Whisper, *"Return me to flow."*

Forgive yourself quickly. Begin again immediately.

God's love is not disappointed in your humanness. It is patient with it, weaving every detour back into purpose.

"My grace is sufficient for you, for My power is made perfect in weakness.", 2 Corinthians 12:9

Weakness is not failure; it is the opening through which strength enters.

Grace as Energy Exchange

Spiritually and scientifically, grace is energy. Every act of kindness, every thought of love, creates measurable energetic resonance in the field around you.

The HeartMath studies reveal that emotions of compassion and care produce coherent waveforms in the heart's electromagnetic field. These waves interact with others' fields, promoting healing, clarity, and peace.

So when you live with intention, you are literally adjusting the energetic weather of your world.

Your grace calms storms you cannot see. Your peace steadies hearts you will never meet.

This is how the circle expands, invisible, constant, sacred.

The Currency of Heaven

In Heaven, the only currency is love. Grace is how it circulates.

Every gift of compassion you give is deposited into the collective treasury of light. From that treasury, blessings flow back into your life in forms beyond comprehension, not as a transaction, but as a continuation.

The universe keeps perfect balance. What you give in love returns multiplied.

This is the law of divine reciprocity. It is not a reward; it is resonance.

"Give, and it will be given to you; a good measure, pressed down, shaken together and running over, will be poured into your lap.", Luke 6:38

The measure you use is vibration, not quantity. When you give joyfully, you receive joyfully. When you give in faith, you receive in faith.

This is how Heaven sustains the rhythm of grace.

Walking as the Circle

To live in the circle of grace is to realize you are never separate from the Source.

You are the channel, the vessel, and the river itself.

When you pray, you inhale grace. When you serve, you exhale it. And as you breathe, you become the rhythm of divine circulation.

The light enters, moves through, and returns to its original point, only to start again.

Prayer of Living Grace

Beloved Source, let me be the open hands through which Your grace flows.

Where there is pain, let me bring comfort. Where there is division, let me bring peace. Where there is need, let me bring generosity.

Remind me that I do not give alone; it is You who gives through me.

May every word I speak and every act I perform extend the circle of Your love until all creation is restored in harmony. Amen.

Reflection

Grace is the unbroken circle of divine energy. It begins in God, flows through you, touches others, and returns to its Source, richer, fuller, more radiant than before.

When you live with awareness, you become that circle, a living embodiment of Heaven's reciprocity.

Every act, every breath, every kindness becomes prayer. Every moment becomes sacred. And the world, through your quiet radiance, remembers that love still moves among us.

THE INFINITE HEART: WHERE TIME AND SPIRIT BECOME ONE

There are truths too vast for the mind, but not too extensive for the heart.

One of them is this: Love does not end. It cannot.

Love is not an emotion; it is energy. It is not memory, it is movement. It is not confined to a moment; it is the timeless pulse of God.

When all things pass, love remains. When bodies fall away, love endures. When voices grow silent, love continues to sing beneath the stillness.

"Love never fails... And now these three remain: faith, hope, and love. But the greatest of these is love.", 1 Corinthians 13:8,13

Love is not the lesson; it is the essence. It is the current that flows through all existence, linking every soul, every life, every atom, in the harmony of eternity.

The Heart Beyond Time

Your heart is not simply an organ. It is a multidimensional instrument, an antenna tuned to divine frequencies.

Science can measure its electromagnetic field, but spirit feels its reach across lifetimes.

Every heartbeat you have ever felt is part of an infinite continuum, a vibration that does not stop when the body ceases. The rhythm changes, but it never disappears.

When someone you love passes, their frequency continues, and your heart, still connected, senses their pulse in subtle ways: a song that stirs you for no reason, a breeze at the right moment, a whisper in your dreams.

These are not memories; they are resonances. Love does not die; it changes form.

You are not remembering them; you are still in conversation with them, soul to soul, heart to heart, frequency to frequency.

The Quantum Continuum of Love

Time, as we know it, is only perception, a river flowing one way for the sake of learning. But in truth, the soul exists outside the river, watching it sparkle from above.

In that eternal dimension, past and future coexist as one. Love transcends sequence; it is the eternal present.

Quantum physics refers to this phenomenon as non-locality, where particles remain connected regardless of distance or time.

Spirit calls it oneness.

When your heart loves, it participates in this cosmic entanglement, forever linked with all it has touched. The vibration of your affection echoes across time and returns amplified, weaving you into the infinite fabric of divine remembrance.

Every prayer you speak, every tear you shed, every act of kindness is recorded not in memory, but in frequency, and that frequency endures forever.

The Heart as Portal

The heart is the meeting point between Heaven and Earth, between seen and unseen.

It is the sacred doorway through which the eternal speaks to the temporal.

When you close your eyes and enter the stillness of your chest, you step outside of time. You can feel everything, your ancestors, your loved ones, your angels, your Creator, not as separate, but as one field of consciousness.

"For where your treasure is, there your heart will be also.", Matthew 6:21

Your treasure is love, and love cannot be lost. Therefore, your heart is never empty.

When you feel grief, you are standing at the threshold of the infinite, longing not for what is gone, but for what is still too vast to comprehend.

And in that longing, you are closer to God than ever.

Eternal Connections

We meet certain souls, lifetime after lifetime, drawn together by resonance. Some come to teach, some to awaken, some to heal wounds carried across generations.

These connections are not coincidences; they are continuations.

When your heart recognizes someone instantly, that is eternity remembering itself. When you forgive sincerely, you heal not only this moment, but many that came before it.

Love's thread weaves through existence like a golden line, each meeting, each parting, another knot tied in the tapestry of divine purpose.

"Before I formed you in the womb I knew you.", Jeremiah 1:5

To know is to recognize, and the soul recognizes across dimensions.

So when you love, you are never beginning. You are continuing.

The Infinite Pulse of the Universe

At the center of creation, there is rhythm, a pulse. It beats in galaxies, in ocean tides, in your chest.

This is the rhythm of the Infinite Heart, the eternal heartbeat of God.

Astrophysicists have discovered that the universe itself hums at frequencies, cosmic background vibrations that never cease.

Scripture has known this all along: *"The heavens declare the glory of God; the skies proclaim the work of His hands."* (Psalm 19:1)

Every vibration of creation is the voice of divine love still speaking.

When you align your heart's frequency with that hum, through prayer, stillness, or compassion, you tune yourself back into the eternal song.

And in that resonance, you find that there is no end, only continuation, transformation, and expansion.

Love's Return

Love always returns to its source. Even when forgotten, it circles back like light finding the break in the clouds.

If you have ever felt abandoned, it is only because love was approaching from a direction you could not yet see.

Grace moves in spirals, not lines. Every heartbreak is a turning point that brings you closer to wholeness.

And when you finally release all resistance, you feel it, the gentle warmth, the invisible embrace, the unmistakable truth that you have never been unloved, not for a single breath of eternity.

The Infinite Christ

Christ is not confined to history. He is the living vibration of love woven through all creation. He exists in every era, in every heart that loves, in every act of forgiveness, in every soul that awakens.

When you love, you meet Him. When you forgive, you become Him. When you breathe in gratitude, you speak His language.

"I am with you always, even to the end of the age. ", Matthew 28:20

Time has no authority over love, and therefore, nothing can separate you from it. Death does not end love; it unveils it. Separation does not break it; it deepens it.

Love is not the echo of God; it is God.

Prayer of the Infinite Heart

Eternal Christ, pulse of all creation, rhythm of all time, I feel You in the silence of my heart.

Teach me to love beyond the boundaries of fear, beyond the illusions of loss.

Let my heart beat in harmony with Yours, until every barrier between Heaven and Earth dissolves.

May my love reach those I cannot touch, heal what I cannot see, and join the great chorus of eternal grace.

Through love, make me infinite. Through peace, make me whole. Through remembrance, make me Yours. Amen.

Reflection

The Infinite Heart is not somewhere above you. It is within you, beating quietly beneath your ribs, connecting you to every soul that ever was or will be.

Every heartbeat you feel is a message from eternity saying: *"You are not alone. You never were. You never will be."*

When you open your heart wide enough, you find that love is not something you send or receive; it is the atmosphere in which you live.

And in that realization, time stops, fear fades, and only God remains.

You are the Infinite Heart, the living bridge between Heaven and Earth, where love, at last, becomes forever.

THE ETERNAL FLAME: LIVING IN THE PRESENCE OF UNBROKEN LOVE

There is a light that no shadow can extinguish. It burns quietly within you, a flame kindled before the foundations of the world, fueled by the breath of God, and sustained by the love of Christ.

You may forget it. You may doubt it. You may walk through years where the wind of sorrow threatens to snuff it out. But it endures. It always endures.

"The light shines in the darkness, and the darkness has not overcome it.", John 1:5

This flame is not a metaphor; it is an essence. It is the vibrational core of who you are, the frequency of divine love in motion, the pulse of eternal life resonating in your chest. It is your connection to God, your remembrance of Heaven, and the quiet assurance that you were never alone, not even in the darkest hour.

The Flame Within

Before you took your first breath, this light lived in you. It is the part of God that said yes when your soul chose to come into being.

It flickers in moments of awe, a sunrise, a song, a child's laughter, a tear that falls not from pain but from recognition.

It brightens when you forgive, when you love without condition, when you speak words that lift others instead of wounding them.

And even when you lose your way, the flame waits patiently beneath the ashes, a single ember of remembrance, ready to ignite again the moment you choose to turn toward love.

You cannot destroy divine fire; you can only forget its warmth.

The Unbreakable Presence

The flame within you is not separate from the flame in Christ. It is the same fire, the living Spirit that flowed through Him, now dwelling in you.

When He said, *"I am the light of the world,"* He also said, *"You are the light of the world."*

The eternal flame does not belong to one; it belongs to all. It is the remarkable continuity of love, the same energy that sparked galaxies, breathed life into dust, and whispered your name into existence.

To live in its presence is to live in remembrance.

You do not have to search for God. You have only to stop running from your own divine reflection. Every heartbeat, every breath, every kind word is the echo of that infinite light.

The Flame and the Breath

Fire cannot live without air. And your soul cannot burn with divine light without Spirit's breath.

The word *"Spirit"* in Hebrew, Ruach, means breath, wind, or movement. Each inhale is an invitation; each exhale, a release. Together they feed the flame.

When you breathe consciously, you participate in the eternal rhythm of creation: inhale, receive love; exhale, give love.

That is prayer in its most natural form. You do not need to speak it aloud. You need only to breathe it.

For as long as you breathe, you are loved. And when your body exhales for the last time, it is not the end of your flame; it is the moment your light rejoins the infinite fire.

The breath of God does not cease; it simply changes direction.

The Flame That Never Fails

Love may seem to fade when life grows heavy. But what fades is only your perception, not the flame itself.

Even when you feel numb, the light burns. Even when you cannot pray, the light intercedes for you. Even when you feel far from grace, grace is already within you, waiting to be seen.

There are moments when loss steals your breath, and the air around you feels hollow, but remember: the fire of love does not die with the body. It is immortal, untouchable, infinite.

The ones you've lost are not gone; they are burning with you, their light joining yours in an unseen constellation of eternal communion.

"Neither death nor life, neither angels nor demons, neither the present nor the future, nor any powers... will be able to separate us from the love of God that is in Christ Jesus our Lord.", Romans 8:38–39

You were never meant to live apart from this flame. You were meant to become it.

Living as Lightbearers

To live as one who carries the eternal flame is to walk gently in a world that has forgotten its own light.

It means forgiving when others cannot. It means offering peace where there is bitterness. It means radiating warmth not from superiority, but from compassion.

You do not have to preach; you only have to shine. People recognize truth not by the words you say, but by the peace they feel in your presence.

This is the way of Christ, to live as a quiet lighthouse in a restless sea.

When you embody love, you remind others of who they are. And in that remembrance, the world heals a little more.

The flame is never meant to be hidden. The candle's purpose is to be seen. And your purpose is to let God's love be visible through your living.

The Science of Eternal Light

Even in science, nothing truly dies. Energy does not vanish; it transforms. The light from distant stars, though their bodies are long gone, still travels across galaxies, ancient photons touching Earth millennia later.

You, too, are made of that same light. Every act of love, every thought of compassion, sends out waves that continue long after your body has moved on. They merge with the vibrations of others, forming an invisible tapestry of grace around the world.

This is eternity in motion, the physics of divine love.

Your flame adds to that brilliance. You are not small in the cosmos; you are the very evidence of its sacred purpose.

The Everlasting Communion

Heaven is not somewhere distant. It is here, in this breath, this heartbeat, this moment. It is the merging of your flame with the infinite, the realization that there was never a divide.

When you love, you open the door. When you forgive, you walk through it. When you live in gratitude, you dwell in the temple of everlasting light.

The eternal flame is not something you visit; it is the home you've never truly left.

And as you live in its glow, you discover that the love you once sought has always been seeking you.

Prayer of the Eternal Flame

Beloved Light of All That Is, kindle my heart anew.

Let every shadow within me become a place where Your fire can shine.

Teach me to walk as one who carries Heaven, to see the sacred in every soul, and never to forget that Your flame is my breath, Your breath my being.

May I be a candle in Your cathedral of creation, a spark that reminds the world of the love that cannot die.

And when my journey here is complete, let my flame join Yours completely, one light, one love, forever burning. Amen.

Reflection

The eternal flame is the final truth of your journey. It is the same truth that began this book: You were never unloved. You were never forsaken. You were never separate.

Love has lived in you from the beginning and will live in you beyond all endings.

You are the light of Christ made manifest, the unbroken echo of God's heartbeat. And as long as love exists, which is to say, forever, so will you.

So let your light shine. Let it rise from the ashes of your doubt, from the quiet corners of your grief, from the sacred center of your heart.

You are the flame that cannot fail, the light that never left, the love that remains.

"For with You is the fountain of life; in Your light we see light.", Psalm 36:9

The story does not end here, because love never ends.

Only light, always light, forever light.

EPILOGUE: THE GREAT CONTINUUM

It begins not in the heavens, but in the quiet pulse of your own heart.

A single beat. A breath that whispers the oldest truth: I never left you.

That was where the first journey began, within the silence, within the ache, within the sacred longing to feel love again. The Heart That Never Left You was that journey inward: a return to the Christ who lives inside every soul, even in the moments we cannot feel His warmth.

But love does not remain contained once it is remembered. Like light, it expands. Like breath, it moves outward. And in its expansion, it becomes revelation.

What once was personal becomes universal. What once was healing becomes creation. And what once was your heartbeat becomes the rhythm of the stars.

When the interstellar traveler **3I/ATLAS** passed through our solar system, it did more than reflect sunlight; it reflected consciousness. It was the universe speaking in its native tongue: motion. Each movement, each orbit, each shimmer of light was a verse in the eternal hymn of God.

Science observed a comet. Spirit recognized a messenger.

As **3I/ATLAS** moved through space, it altered fields, awakened frequencies, and reminded creation of its divine rhythm. It carried with it the same energy that breathes through galaxies, the same intelligence that stirs the tides of emotion, the same love that whispered through time, *"You are not alone."*

The message of The Heart That Never Left You was about rediscovering the Christ within. The message of The Messenger of Light is about seeing that same Christ reflected in the cosmos.

One spoke of the inner universe, the sacred temple of flesh and faith where Jesus' presence abides. The other reveals the outer universe, the vast cathedral of stars where His vibration sings across eternity.

Together, they form the Great Continuum: the endless flow of love through every form of existence.

Everything that moves is alive. Everything that shines is part of the same eternal body. The light in your eyes and the light that crosses the sky are not different; they are expressions of one radiance.

The same vibration that holds galaxies in motion beats within your chest. The exact frequency that lifted **3I/ATLAS** from the depths of interstellar darkness carries your soul toward awakening.

When heaven moves, Earth responds. When you love, the cosmos brightens. When you forgive, the field of creation harmonizes.

You are not separate from the stars. You are their continuation.

"In Him all things hold together.", Colossians 1:17

The Christ within you is the Christ of the cosmos, the living resonance of all that was, is, and will ever be.

The planets orbit not by chance, but by grace. The comets travel not randomly, but purposefully. The soul awakens not accidentally, but divinely.

Each orbit, each breath, each heartbeat belongs to the same pulse, the rhythm of an infinite Creator loving Himself through creation.

3I/ATLAS came and went as all visitors do, but its message remains:

That we, too, are travelers of light. That love moves through us as through the stars. That every ending is merely another beginning in a continuum without boundaries.

Its path through our skies mirrored your path through life, drawn from Source, transformed by light, leaving trails of illumination for others to follow. It did not linger, because light never clings; it simply moves, faithfully, eternally, beautifully, on its way back home.

So let this be the closing and the beginning all at once:

The Heart That Never Left You is the same love that called the stars into being. The Messenger of Light is the same Christ whose radiance awakens every soul.

Two stories, one truth. Two journeys, one destination. Two flames, one fire, the infinite love of God made visible in both heart and heaven.

When you next look to the night sky, know that it is looking back at you. For the universe does not exist above you, it exists through you.

You are part of its divine design. You are its awareness, its expression, its song.

Every photon, every breath, every prayer, all returning to the exact center, the same light, the same Love.

And thus, the Great Continuum is revealed: Love within, Love without, Love unbroken, Love eternal.

It is the breath of God in motion, the pulse of Christ through creation, the radiant journey of every soul remembering home.

The comet was never a stranger. It was a reflection, a reminder from the cosmos that the same flame guiding its path is the one that burns forever inside you.

"The heavens declare the glory of God; the skies proclaim the work of His hands. ", Psalm 19:1

The Great Continuum The same light that moves through the stars moves through you. The same grace that holds the planets together holds your heart. The same eternal Christ who breathed galaxies into motion still whispers your name, in every dawn, every silence, every shining thing.

You are not simply part of the universe. You are its continuation, its remembrance, its messenger of light.

AUTHOR'S NOTE

A CLOSING REFLECTION FROM TINA KETCH

To those who have walked this journey with me, thank you.

Thank you for reading, for feeling, for opening your heart to love's unending call. Whether you came to these pages searching for comfort, curiosity, or understanding, know this: the very act of reaching toward light means you already carry it.

Writing The Heart That Never Left You was the beginning of a revelation, that love, even when it feels absent, never truly departs. Writing The Messenger of Light became its continuation, a widening of that revelation into the stars themselves, where divine presence shines through the language of vibration and motion.

Both books were written in awe, one for the sacred heart within us, the other for the radiant cosmos around us. But together, they became a mirror: a reflection of how the human soul and the living universe echo the same song of remembrance.

I believe we are all travelers of light. Some of us journey inward, seeking peace in silence. Others journey outward, seeking understanding in the vastness of creation. But in truth, both paths lead home, to the same eternal presence, the same Christ energy, the same love that moves through all things.

May these words remind you that your light matters. Your breath matters. Your journey matters.

You are the continuation of creation, a note in God's eternal melody, a spark in His infinite flame, a messenger of His unending love.

As you close this book, may you never again feel distant from the divine, for you are the very expression of it.

And when you lift your eyes to the heavens, may you know, deeply, peacefully, joyfully, that the same force guiding the stars is guiding you, too.

With gratitude, reverence, and endless light

- Tina Ketch

www.ingramcontent.com/pod-product-compliance
Lightning Source LLC
LaVergne TN
LVHW020711110826
845149LV00012B/2205